'What a joy to read Campbell's work Varieties of Hope which, once again, demonstrates the originality of her thinking and the depth of her understanding of the human condition. Her writing does not just evidence the breadth of her knowledge, as she effortlessly moves between literary criticism and psychoanalytic theory but is driven by a desire to shed light on the intractable human dilemmas encountered in the consulting room. Radical, political and clinical this is a book for our time, exploring the very theme that eludes us most today. Campbell's work helps keep hope alive.'

Pamela Howard, *CPsychol, UKCP reg psychoanalytic psychotherapist, programme director, Counselling and Psychotherapy, principal lecturer in Psychotherapy, School of Humanities and Social Science, University of Brighton*

'One of the best compliments it is possible to pay a writer, or therapist for that matter, is "Well, I never thought of it that way before". This collection of essays by Jan Campbell leads the reader to precisely that sentiment time and again. Hope is a vital component in human affairs. Campbell's exploration of hope, its varieties and its subterfuges, considers what literature and psychoanalysis can tell us about hope under attrition and its capacities for regeneration. Perhaps not paradoxically, Campbell's themes occupy the shadow side of contemporary politics and culture, including some of its major legal and medical controversies. It is a commonplace to say this or that book is timely – though this one undoubtedly is. Some varieties of hope, after all, are simply better and more pressing than others. As we are constantly being told, and not for the first time, hope is in short supply. And in that "and not for the first time", perhaps, lies a source of hope in itself.'

Roger Lippin, *psychoanalytic psychotherapist and supervisor (UKCP registered), M.Sc., C.Q.S.W*

Varieties of Hope

This book explores how hope operates as an ambivalent force in relation to issues of sex and gender, power and identity in both our private and public lives.

The author blends her deep knowledge of psychotherapy and mental health with cultural and philosophical understanding to consider how we have reached our current dilemmas around sex and gender, race, power and identity. Psychoanalysis is put to task in relation to clinical practice, literature, feminism, politics and the understandings of how our personal lives and selves interact with the wider cultural moment we are living through. She explores these issues with compassion and understanding and offers a vision of how we may be able to navigate through widely varying perspectives to a new way of envisioning hope today, as both a false promise and a real and necessary component in our lives and within the clinical encounter.

Drawing on clinical psychoanalytic work as well as literature and memoir, this is essential reading for anyone wanting a psychoanalytically informed understanding of where society is on key issues and where we may be able to get to with hope.

Jan Campbell trained as a psychoanalyst and psychotherapist at the Guild of Psychotherapists, qualifying in 2002. Since then she has worked in private practice. She has also had a career as a literary academic, working at the Cultural Studies Department at the University of Birmingham until 2002, and after it was closed as a Reader in English literature and psychoanalysis in the English Department. She retired as an academic in 2013 due to ill health. Campbell is the author of several books on psychoanalysis and culture; her books have focused on psychoanalysis in relation to feminism, film, autobiography, time and most recently on motherhood and telepathy.

Varieties of Hope
Stories of Sexuality, Shame and Power

Jan Campbell

Routledge
Taylor & Francis Group

LONDON AND NEW YORK

Designed cover image: Getty Images

First published 2026
by Routledge
4 Park Square, Milton Park, Abingdon, Oxon OX14 4RN

and by Routledge
605 Third Avenue, New York, NY 10158

Routledge is an imprint of the Taylor & Francis Group, an informa business

British Library Cataloguing-in-Publication Data
A catalogue record for this book is available from the British Library

Library of Congress Cataloging-in-Publication Data
A catalog record has been requested for this book

ISBN: 978-1-032-84952-2 (hbk)
ISBN: 978-1-032-84951-5 (pbk)
ISBN: 978-1-003-51577-7 (ebk)

DOI: 10.4324/9781003515777

Typeset in Sabon
by Taylor & Francis Books

For Esme

Contents

Foreword

When Freud formulated on various occasions what he took to be the aims of psychoanalytic treatment he offered us what he took to be a sliding scale of hope. At his most optimistic he famously suggested that 'where id was, there ego should be', that we were able to acknowledge, appropriate and use for our own satisfaction what had hitherto been unconscious thoughts and desires; through psychoanalysis, he claimed, we may even recover our apparently innate capacity to 'love and work'. But more often than not Freud would be prone to write more ironically – the aim of psychoanalysis was to drive the horse in the direction the horse wants to go – or more conventionally, or 'realistically' – he would insist that the 'ego is not master in his own house', that we had little or no power in or over our own lives; that there was no necessary connection between what we wanted, and thought we wanted, and what we could have. That our satisfaction was precarious, not simply there for the taking.

Once Freud realised that wishing was at the very heart of our lives, hope was the first casualty. What we wanted and were looking forward to – the sustaining enjoyments of our lives – was, sometimes reassuringly, wildly unrealistic. And the question was what kind of terms we could come to about this, in Freud's view, fundamental predicament. As Jan Campbell makes clear in this remarkable, and remarkably original, book, hope needs to be radically redescribed if it is to have a place in the theory and practice of psychoanalysis. But then what, after all, would be the point of a psychoanalysis with such an impoverished view of hope? Psychoanalysis often has to work hard not to be more of the problem it is claiming to treat.

Hope became suspiciously wishful in psychoanalysis as Freud discovered that we were essentially ambivalent and wishful creatures, trying to wish away our ambivalence, our desire, our unconsciousness: our fear of ourselves and of other people. Freud, that is to say, was engaged through his psychoanalytic writing, in exposing hoping as the most omniscient thing we ever do: hoping as, in the language of psycho-analysis, that most absurd and inevitable thing, our attempt not only to predict the future, but to predict a future that we could want. That the future could be better than the past was the fundamental belief that justified and legitimated psychoanalytic treatment. And yet as psycho-analysis developed Freud's radical and unrelenting anti-utopianism set profound limits to human possibility and potential. The only way we know if something is true, the American pragmatist philosopher Richard Rorty wrote, is if it helps us get the life we want. Freud's story about the unconscious radically complicated any idea we might have about the life we want (or think we want), and indeed any idea we might have about the truth. The life we want, which is the life we are hoping for, is both an inevitable preoccupation and a preoccupation that psychoanalysis ineluctably ironises.

It was the plausibility of autonomy and the limits to self-knowledge that Freud was increasingly impressed by. The modern individual, in Freud's account, lived in a disarray of largely unconscious conflicting and unacceptable desires. She could neither be at peace with herself, nor give a coherent account of herself. Her history and her desires, and her history of her desires, were beyond her. Even in his earliest work (*The Studies in Hysteria*, 1895), which he wrote with Joseph Breuer, he would write that that the aim of therapy they were inventing was the trans-forming of hysterical misery into common human unhappiness. Clearly, when it comes to psychoanalysis, we shouldn't get our hopes up. But as Campbell's winning and understated title suggests, hope comes in many forms, and the impoverished forms of hope we find in psychoanalysis may be saying more about psychoanalysis as traditionally conceived than about the varieties of hope. Freud may have as she puts it, 'also hated hope' but she can also love Freud's pessimism and love hope, and this makes Campbell's version of psychoanalysis the more ample thing it is too often shying away from being. That you can love hope and pessi-mism is the point of and the pleasure of Campbell's expansive book, expansiveness not being the thing we tend to associate with psycho-analytical writing. We have not been encouraged to think of psycho-analysts as the 'visionary company' that they might be.

The languages of psychoanalysis – at least prior to Campbell's book – have been inhospitable to the pleasures and the possibilities of hope (another word for hope is vision). After Freud, it has been Winnicott's account of a non-compliant life, and to Lacan's account of the ethical 'act' in which one refuses to cede one's desire, that we have to go to for a psychoanalytical account of any kind of real hope or freedom, or inspiration. They show us, as does Campbell in her own idiosyncratic way, that if improvisation is our only hope – improvisation within our supposed constraints, within our available theories and practices – it has large and unpredictable consequences. What Campbell is after in this book is what she calls a 'reasonable case for hope', but with her own particular flair, that is neither unreasonable nor dutifully or unduly constrained. In her searing and compassionate critiques of Klein's foundational theory of reparation, or of the determined and scandalous misrecognition and mal-treatment of ME sufferers, or her subtle and searching redescriptions of shame and sadomasochism, in psychoanalytical theory and clinical work, we see that rare thing – an undogmatic curiosity and commitment to the possibilities in a lived life. What Campbell's book shows us, in no uncertain or unnuanced terms, is that hope need be neither, merely wishful, nor forbidden, nor naïve, nor turned into a phobic object in the language of psychoanalysis. Because hope and variety go together there is a lot more to say and write about both them. After reading Campbell's book we can see how psychoanalysis might help us to do this.

Adam Phillips

Acknowledgements

I would like to thank Roger Lippen for all our discussions, and the pleasure I have had through our mutual love of literature; your enthusiasm for my writing has meant so much. I am also deeply grateful to Adam Phillips for all our conversations about psychoanalysis, for reading drafts of this book and for his encouragement for me write again, which worked! Many thanks to Pam Howard, for all our years of companionship inside and outside of psychoanalysis. Thanks to my friends, especially to Erica Carter, Ros Lopez and Debbie Friedman for precious time spent together. Thanks also to Kate Hawes, my publisher, for her enthusiasm for the project, and Aakriti Aggarwal for her help with editing the manuscript.

To my doctors and health practitioners, I would like to thank Sarah Myhill, who helped me with my myalgic encephalomyelitis (ME) when I was most lost; my Chinese herbalist Andrew Flowers; and to my most wonderful lung consultant Katie Hurt, for her calm, laser-like attention whenever I get really sick, and for being the epitome of what NHS care should consist of. Huge thanks also to my daughter Esme and her partner Daniel Coleman and baby Finn, for the joy and happiness they bring me.

Finally, I would like to express my love and gratitude to my partner Mike Van Duuren for his kindness, humour, his superb talent in cooking delicious food and all our years together; for his unstinting love in the face of the twists and turns of my journey through illness; and for being essential in the partial recovery from my ME. Without you, this book would never have been written.

1 Varieties of Hope

We live, deaf to the ground beneath us,
Ten steps away no one hears our speeches,

But where there's so much as half a conversation
The Kremlin's mountaineer will get his mention.

His fingers are fat as grubs
And the words, final as lead weights, fall from his lips,

His cockroach whiskers leer
And his boot tops gleam.

Around him a rabble of thin-necked leaders-
Fawning half-men for him to play with,

They whinny, purr or whine
As he prates and points a finger,

One by one forging his laws, to be flung
Like horseshoes at the head, the eye or the groin,

And every killing is a treat
For the broad chested Ossette.

('Epigram to Stalin' by Osip Mandelstam,
November 1933)[1]

In her truly heroic account of trying to save her husband, and when that failed, his poetry, Nadezhda Mandelstam gives a terrifying portrayal of both the necessity and folly of hope. *Hope against Hope* (1999) is Nadezhda's memoir of her life with Osip after the creation of his poem

DOI: 10.4324/9781003515777-1

against Stalin, which was not written down on paper. Even so, just the hearsay of its existence was enough to be a death sentence. The persecution of artists and poets by Stalin's exterminating forces from the 1930s onwards is well known. Virtually anyone could be exiled to labour camps or Gulags, for doing anything. Being denounced was often all it took and if prisoners returned from exile, they were often re-arrested and sent away again. It was a regime pf psychological terror. First, the knock on the door from the interrogators, 'Suddenly about one o'clock in the morning, there was a sharp explicit knock on the door. "They've come for Osip", I said and went to open the door' (Mandelstam, 1999, p. 4). And then the 'suspect' would be taken away for interrogation, which was constituted mainly of psychological torture. The aim of Stalin's terror was to destroy a person's mind, to the extent that the later physical death was practically immaterial. Osip is tortured and indeed begins to lose his mind. After Osip's interrogation and torture, he is sent away into exile with his wife. Being given permission for Nadezhda to accompany Osip was seen as an act of mercy. Away in the country, Nadezhda suffers bouts of typhus and dysentery, whilst Osip suffers bouts of insanity. Interestingly, it is only when Osip is mad that he can understand the true horror of his situation. In these states he keeps imagining his imminent execution. When Osip is sane again, he begins to hope. One of the many extraordinary things about Nadezhda's memoir is this cycle of hope that many people under Stalin's power were destined to suffer. The paradox of hope in Osip's madness, and indeed within the whole story, is that when he is delusional, Osip recognises the danger he is in and fantasises about his impending execution. He even jumps out of the window, in an attempt to kill himself, whilst in hospital. However, when Osip returns to sanity, he connects with the false illusion that he is safe. In a paranoid moment Osip imagines a group of workers are going to grab him when he least expects it. But as Nadezhda points out, 'This is indeed what happens four years later'. She writes: In his dementia M [Osip] understood perfectly well what was coming, but when he recovered he lost this sense of reality and began to believe he was safe' (Mandelstam, 1999, p. 58).

Stalin was envious, we could say particularly envious of Mandelstam because he regarded the poet as a genius. And so integral to the torture and exile was the intention, the guards told Nadezhda, to 'isolate and preserve' Osip. Stalin's habit of playing with his victims, seemingly extending clemency and then killing them, or giving people hope only to have it time upon time vanish beneath their feet, is something that *Hope against Hope* eloquently depicts again and again.

With the story of the Mandelstams and the poem against Stalin, it is apt to remember now how we are living through another 'mountaineer' living in the Kremlin, and the necessity of hope and its folly lies everywhere. In a world now where arguably socialism as a utopia can never happen because utopias are built on the concept of limitless time in the future, a becoming. Climate change decrees that this utopian sense of time is obsolete. The time of the world is ending, finite, so a socialist utopia is impossible. All we can envisage are the possibilities within that circumscribed future. Without hope, life is not just unbearable, it is impossible. Nadezhda describes the moment when she is confronted by this annulment of hope when she and her husband are politely put on a train to exile; in comfort surrounded by guards. Their two brothers, her brother and brother-in law have accompanied them and are waiting outside the train window, but the couple are not allowed to open the window to say goodbye. It is in this moment that hope vanishes for Nadezhda and she tries to put into words the psychological dislocation that happens to people who cross this 'fateful line':

> At the moment when I entered the coach and saw our brothers through the glass, my world split into two halves. Everything that had previously existed now vanished to become a dim memory, something beyond the looking glass, and the future opening up before me no longer meshed with the past. Its first result was utter indifference to what we had left behind – an indifference due to our knowledge that we had all set out on a path of inescapable doom. One of us might be granted a week's grace, even a year, but the end would be the same. It would be the end of everything – friends, relatives, my mother, Europe.
>
> (Mandelstam, 1999, p. 42)

Stalin was a torturer or sadist driven by envy, and he poisoned the people he destroyed by false hope. Anyone who is the least bit romantic about socialism with communist roots should read *Hope against Hope*; it is lesson to all of us in the way it shows us how truly unbearable it is to live in a world where all realistic hope has been corrupted. Perhaps what is most frightening is not just that sadism corrupts the torturer; we can swallow that, and we know it's true, if not from experience, then from the stories, history tells us. But the unpalatable truth that being persecuted can also corrupt people, that is harder to accept.

Stalin's torture of his subjects is on a grand scale what domestic abusers do to their victims on an everyday basis. Probably as an analyst I understand much more clearly what happens to women (and it is mainly women) who are victimised in this way, because they are the patients that find their way into my consulting room. For the women it is a kind of addiction, they become a sort of slave to their male abuser, trying to transform him with the power of their love. But the abuse, which can often go on for twenty, thirty years or more, is a kind of takeover of the women's personality and identity. The man, who is very narcissistic and controlling, will make the woman work in all sorts of ways to please him, through domestic chores, sexual pleasure, etc. He will take control over minute and personal aspects of the woman's life, like choosing her clothes and jewellery. One woman I saw could never go out with any feeling of safety because she couldn't unlock the front door from the outside. Her husband had installed a special lock which meant she had to always be in in case he came home, or if she went out and he was unhappy he would lock her out from the inside.

Another woman could never choose her own clothes as they had to be ones that pleased her husband. She would talk of the frantic attempts to please this monster of a man, in how she looked constantly for a sign of acknowledgement in the witty conversation she would strike up, or the things she would buy for the house to impress him. He worked in interior design. She was always searching and hoping for a glimmer of approval or kindness, and then she could relax that things would be alright and that she was safe. Women in these situations live in daily terror, and yet they are not weak. On the contrary they are often extremely strong and resilient. We could think that this is madness, and ask how could a woman live like this for even two weeks, let alone the twenty or so years she had actually endured with him? And yet the horror of this coercive control or psychological torture is that it works like a kind of hypnosis or brainwashing. A woman speaking many years after she had left her abuser, said that it had been a kind of addiction or trauma bond filled with continual hope alternating with fear. As Spinoza tells us fear and hope are two sides of the same coin, 'fear cannot be without hope nor hope without fear'. Two sides of life perhaps? Especially, for a world narrowing because of terror. Because the absolute beyond of hope is its abandonment. Nadezhda describes this moment when her life splits into two through the train glass, as a moment of doom, the world as she has known it coming abruptly to an end:

> Until a short time before, I had been full of concern for all my friends and relatives, for my work, for everything I set store by. Now this concern was gone – and fear, too. Instead there was an acute sense of being doomed – it was this that gave rise to an indifference so overwhelming as to be almost physical, like a heavy weight pressing down on the shoulders, I also felt that time, as such had come to an end – there was only an interlude before the inescapable swallowed us ...

How would it come the inescapable? Where, and in what form? It really didn't matter. Resistance was useless. Having entered a realm of non-being, I had lost the sense of death. In the face of doom, even. Fear disappears. Fear is a gleam of hope, the will to live, self-assertion. ... Fear and hope are bound up with each other. Losing hope, we lose fear as well – there is nothing to be afraid for.

(Mandelstam, 1999, p. 42)

I have come across this sense of being doomed quite rarely in clinical practice, but I have come across it, and it is nothing to do with being ordinarily depressed. Depression is a damping down of our conflicts; Winnicott called it 'fog on the battlefield', but it is not the same feeling of doom you have when life as you know it and everyone in it has ceased to exist. I have come across this feeling in parents whose children have died, and I have also encountered it in some women who were severely sexually abused for most of their childhood. In short, the devastation we can feel when everything meaningful, all concerns have dissipated. Then, perhaps, as Nadezhda so vividly portrays, hope is extinguished along with any point in remaining alive.

So, hope is essential to life, and yet is gets so easily perverted or harnessed in ways that aren't really good for us. In other words, there are varieties of hope, and some flavours or types are perhaps better than others. The kind of poisonous hope utilised by Stalin, or by domestic abusers is enough to destroy hope and at least all psychological aliveness. But what is hope for the good or hope that is nourishing for us? Maybe hope is difficult to think about it because it is so easy to idealise or sentimentalise. Indeed, Freud thought the hope vested in religion to be nothing more than a childish illusion of helplessness and the need for protection placed on an almighty father. We might think that's too easy a dismissal of spirituality that gives immense value and purpose to many societies and cultures. And yet Freud's *Future of an Illusion* (Freud, 1927) poses a question, about hope and civilisation. What do we do, when our hopes individually and collectively are that badly threatened? How, do we comprehend the climate catastrophe we are facing? How do we deal in an ever-increasing globalised world of late capitalism, with the wealth inequality, the wars and conflicts, the mass migration and the government corruption or autocracy, that seems to define living in a modern age. How do we expect or even ask our children to cope with the end of a world, our world which is dying, one in which we have been, at the very least, complicit in destroying?

Freud's pessimism, his *Civilisation and Its Discontents* (Freud, 1929) written just after *Future of an Illusion*, is his insistence on the reality principle. The destructiveness of people's drives, and the guilt engendered by self and society. The best we can hope for is common misery delivering us from neurosis. I love Freud's pessimism, his clarity about the evil, the deprivation of others, and violence, people can achieve from simply the bed of their own narcissism. But I also think Freud hated hope as he saw it simply as wish fulfilment and idealisation, in other words – fantasy. He always wanted to put the brakes on hope because he saw it as a defence against the unavoidable ambivalence of the human condition. I think this is important; but surely, we can add hope to psychoanalysis in a way that doesn't compromise ambivalence or reality? Is that possible? Let's look at some of the people that have tried.

One of the most surprising things about searching for an understanding or appreciation of the value of hope in psychoanalysis is that it doesn't really exist. More often, than not, where it does exist it is seen as a pathology. Freud, Klein and Lacan and the theories they inspire, all see hope as a poisonous variety. Something which provides false illusions that stay or keep us from finding necessary desire and accepting reality. Harold Boris, in his remarkable book *Envy*, is an exception (Boris, 1994). Not that he sees hope as anything positive, for he too, sees hope as something that holds back actualising growth and change, but he at least gives hope the due significance it deserves, in being discussed or thought about. For Boris, hope is part of an early selection process that he links to Darwinian theory. Instead of the life and death drives, Boris understands a duality of the life drives with a selection principle that harks back to the beginning of life. We are born with an ability to select or choose, and this is where hope arrives as an early preconception. These inclinations become filled out as the hopes and wishes we develop with, and which are then followed through to an imagined future. For Boris the baby can desire and receive succour and satisfaction from the breast, but there is something else, the recognition that the breast does not belong to the baby: 'When it occurs to baby that the breast, through provident and regularly nurturant, is nevertheless not his, a crisis – the so called anaclitic depression – takes place' (Boris, 1994, p. 7). This dependent outrage of losing has nothing to do with satisfaction or weaning, it is a crisis of ownership. The breast, which is hoped belongs to the baby, in actuality is attached to someone else. However, much desire and satiation the baby feels at the breast, the pain that is heralded in the sudden understanding that the breast is not owned, ushers in, according to Boris an acute state of envy.

For hope, is always on the side of the selection principle, and as such is closely linked to Freud's self-preservative drives. Thus, hope becomes attached to our ego ideals and is always predicated on a permanently elongated future. Whom we might be. What we might have. Boris talks about the hope of a straight man in finding 'Miss Right', whereas 'Miss Right Now' is the actual desire (Boris, 1994, pp. 58–59). Hope, then, is our earliest selection or choice, and it is easy to see how if fantasies of hope and what is finest, are too dominant, then actual desire can't get a foothold.

I want to think about this choosiness or hope in relation to women's desire. Some women can fall in love with quite narcissistic or even cruel men and then hope, against the odds, to change them with the strength of their love. This is often why women remain with abusive partners, there is a perverse desire to heal the man through loving him as a kind of child. Its perverse because it never works and becomes both destructive and addictive. Or women can in their heads, and in their hope, not want sex with their male partner, only to find they really enjoy it with their bodies – that is experience real desire – when it actually happens. Of course, there are plenty of other reasons women might not want sex, like being angry or tired or not attracted. And yet when it is a refusal that is so contradicted by the desire these women go on to feel in the experience of sex, then the inhibiting thoughts can be seen as the kind of hope or choosiness Boris is describing. Men and women can have very romantic ideas or fantasies of whom they want to fall in love with; these hopes are reminiscent of earlier parental ideals, but for desire to work, for a lover to be realised, these hopes can't be too similar or locked into early parental ideals if they are to make way for the immediacy and difference of desire.

Desire for men (and sometimes for women), on the other hand, can be totally split off from any kind of selective ideals. This desire becomes a different route or sexual perversion where emotions and intimacy, familiar feelings of affection are totally missing. Boris writes: 'Hope holds desire from taking its any old course of least resistance and it keeps desire from static satiety by calling it to finer possibilities (Boris, 1994, p. 10).

We could think of this with regard to Freud, where hope translates as the wish fulfilment linked to our incestuous ties, that has to be moved towards reality, for its fulfilment as desire. In a remarkable albeit short paper called 'On the Universal Tendency to Debasement in the Sphere of Love' (Freud, 1912, pp. 177–190), Freud contrasts two currents of affection and sexuality that have to be brought together to sustain happy love. In this paper, Freud describes a fundamental ambivalence to sexual desire that exists in all of us. We start in life with affectionate ties to parents, that quickly become complicated by more sensual wanting, Freud's infantile sexuality. This conflict between affection and desire takes on a new tension in adolescence when fully fledged sexuality takes hold. Here, men and women split off affection from desire in attempt to deal with the original incestuous object. Men split their desire between the incestuous object that they overvalue and love, and a sexual object they feel sexually free with. The famous Madonna/Whore division. Whilst women, who are more tied to their incestuous links (through mothering), don't debase men in the same way. They are more affectionate and loving, but their sex drive remains more prohibited and sublimated through romantic fantasy. Thus, women fantasise about sex with men they can't have, but don't actually want the man in their bed.

We might consider today that this splitting in sexual difference is old-fashioned and plenty of women debase their sexual objects, and plenty of men fantasise about women they can't have. And yet Freud's paper is compelling in asking us to confront the essential dilemma for people, that 'where they love, they do not desire, and where they desire, they cannot love' (Freud, 1912, p. 185). If we think about this ambivalence between affection and sex in terms of the relationship between hope and desire; we can see that hope, as part of the incestuous sacred bond with an ideal parent or ego, is filled with what we fantasise about and aesthetically select. The danger of a predominance of hope is that it runs out, thus no intimacy in a sexual way can really happen. Whereas the reality of desire, once it becomes split off or separated from the affectionate and hopeful bonds, becomes debased and violent, in all the ways for example sexual misogyny operates towards women.

So, we can open out the ambivalence we all feel about sex and love into a wider discussion of how hope and desire both operate within society. And perhaps this is why hope is such a difficult thing to think about without reducing it to sentimentalisation and idealistic fantasy. In *Hope Against Hope*, we see false hope becoming a kind of masochistic and childish regression, that the community is forced to adopt in the face of widespread terror. The poet Mandelstam had a habit, according to his wife, of idealising the nineteenth century: 'At the beginning of the thirties, M once said to me: "You know, if ever there was a golden age, it was the nineteenth century. Only we didn't know"' (Mandelstam, 1999, p. 253).

If we read Dickens, we are bound to disagree. Given the brutality and bleakness that was inextricably the life of the Mandelstams in Soviet Russia, it's easy to see how the traditions of democracy and humanism that stemmed from the nineteenth century were turned into an illusion of that period as a 'golden age'. We could reflect on how Marxism and socialism have always been an ideology of hope that has failed in its meeting with reality. If hope lives on in Christianity as the suffering we endure, like Christ, to join him in an afterlife as glory, then hope in more secular histories has a more pessimistic bent. For George Steiner, tragedy is the truth marred by hope's triviality. And for Walter Benjamin, it's our pessimism, our melancholy in the face of history's progress, that we must adhere to. These thinkers are echoed in an article in *The New Statesman* called 'The New Age of Tragedy', by Robert D. Kaplan, John Gray and Helen Thompson. They argue that our instable, conflictual and chaotic world, cannot be saved by hopeful idealism in human agency and liberal ideology. Instead, we have to become tragic realists about tragedy, we have to be disappointed, fearful of the worst, and yet undaunted by the task we face. Gray's point, in particular, is noteworthy:

> The reality of a planet from which there is no exit is intensifying competition for control of its resources. Ukraine is not only the world's breadbasket but a rich site of rare earths, while the Russian-occupied territories of Donetsk and Luhansk contain substantial deposits of shale gas. Geology and geography shape our conflicts as profoundly as any clash between autocracy and democracy. If there is hope, it is in recognising this fact.
>
> (John Gray in Kaplan et al., 2023)

Of course, on some level these thinkers are right, Putin's terror isn't going to listen to liberals like us, but is tragic realism really that realistic? Isn't tragedy full of delusional melodrama? I know trauma is. And tragedy is always, whatever else it is, an exciting drama. Just think of King Lear's madness, or Putin's for that matter. We can't have reality without some component of delusion and illusion. As Winnicott shows us, we can only really bear reality on the basis of the illusion that meets it. Where does that leave hope? What hope is there for hope in other words?

What's really interesting in Gray's analysis is the reciprocity he alludes to, which is materially built into our world, whatever its dysfunction. Dickens wrote the history of the nineteenth century as tragedy, as a melodrama, but with a humour and psychological insight that saves us from any simple explanation of the human condition. Dickens was well aware of the poisonous nature of hope, but he also knew that there is literally nothing for us in the world without it. For Dickens the reciprocity of life, and the characters within it, is worth exploring. Perhaps Dickens's novels are some kind of answer to Kafka's hilarious quote, there 'is plenty of hope, an infinite amount of hope – but not for us'.[2]

Pip, in *Great Expectations* (Dickens, 1996), has great hopes and expectations to become a gentleman. The novel is about the tragedy of hope that abounds for most of the participants. Pip's ambitions to become a gentleman and his ardent but impossible love for Estella colour and drive the plot. Hope is also its inevitable failure without any true meeting place with reality. We find this embodied in the truly terrifying figure of Miss Havisham, who lures and buys Pip into a middle-class world, teaching him to become a gentleman and to fall in love with her adopted daughter Estella, whom she has schooled to break men's hearts. Like Stalin, Miss Havisham, who has been traumatised by being jilted at the altar, stops time through a hope or a hopelessness that refuses to be defeated. Miss Havisham in her horrific faded wedding gown and cobwebby mansion, left exactly as it was when the rejection happened, represents not just trauma's refusal to move in time and move on; but a kind of revenge reminiscent of Stalin or a domestic abuser, where she sadistically plays with Pip and Estella. The game Miss Havisham sets up between them is to watch Pip's hope, and hopeless love for Estella, break on the rocks of his ambition to win her and a life worthy of his illusions.

Hurting Pip, as retribution for the wound she has received, is Miss Havisham's hope, and this becomes orchestrated as a malevolent desire in making Pip fall in love with Estella, the adopted daughter who has been schooled into being heartless.

> Estella was always about, and always let me in and out, but never told me I might kiss her again. Sometimes, she would coldly tolerate me; sometimes, she would condescend to me, sometimes she would be quite familiar with me; sometimes, she would tell me energetically that she hated me. Miss Havisham would often ask me in a whisper, or when we were alone, 'Does she grow prettier and prettier, Pip?' And when I said yes (for indeed she did), would seem to enjoy it greedily. Also when I played at cards Miss Havisham would embrace her with lavish fondness, murmuring something in her ear that sounded like 'Break their hearts my pride and hope, break their hearts and have no mercy!'
>
> (Dickens, 1996, p. 95)

Pip's hope for Estella is utterly hopeless as she has no heart, and no feelings. It is no surprise that she ends up in a sadomasochistic relationship with the repulsive and cruel Bentley Drummel who beats her. When Pip eventually confesses his love to Estella, he admits his failure: 'I know. I have no hope that I shall ever call you mine, Estella. ... Still I love you' (Dickens, 1996, p. 362).

Unmoved, Estella can't understand what Pip is talking about, except on an intellectual level. it's not a question of whether she can love him, for she can't love anyone:

> that there are sentiments, fancies — I don't know what to call them — which I am not able to comprehend. When you say you love me, I know what you mean, as a form of words, but nothing more. You address nothing in my breast, you touch nothing there. I don't care for what you say at all. I have tried to warn you of this; now, have I not.
>
> (Dickens, 1996, p. 362)

Pip's hope for Estella is arguably an intense romantic longing or fantasy that can't materialise into actual desire because the woman he adores is indifferent to him. This is more like Freud's idea of the women's ability to have desire only if the object is prohibited, which pretty much defined his understanding of hysteria. So, Pip's hysterical desire for Estella is matched by her equally hopeless inability to have feelings. In this she shares Miss Havisham's ego ideal, contemptuous of men, and cold. In a perverse twist, Estella and Miss Havisham's ideal is of a vindictive woman/mother, not a saintly one, bent on revenge and the denigration of men. If Pip's hysterical love fits a more feminine stereotype, then Estella's mimicry of what the older woman has taught her mirrors a sort of cruel, narcissistic perfection, which is also associated with certain men's denigration of women. Perhaps Dickens is reminding us that in the tendency to universal debasement in the sphere of love (to borrow Freud's wording) men and women swap over in terms of their splitting between hope and desire. We could say where some people hope they do not desire, and where they desire, they cannot hope. Of course, Dickens is also gesturing to the universal debasement in the sphere of class relations. Pip's encounters with Estella and Miss Havisham make him ashamed of his clothes, his manners, his home:

> I had believed in the kitchen as a chaste though not magnificent apartment; I had believed in the forge as the glowing road to manhood and independence. Within a single year all this was changed. Now, it was all coarse and common.
>
> (Dickens, 1996, p. 72)

Pip's response to this shame are his ideals of hope, his great expectations of life and love which are extremely and determinedly followed in the novel. Eventually they are dashed, not just by the cold-hearted Estella, but by Pip's disillusionment of middle-class status and riches. The world of gentlemen that he succeeds in inhabiting is debauched, untrue and bitterly disappointing. In wanting the very best ego ideals for himself, Pip betrays his moral centre. It is only when Pip realises that it is Magwitch (the convict) who is his benefactor, not Miss Havisham who was always an unlikely fairy godmother, that things change. David Trotter argues that this moral revision replaces Pip's desire with guilt. And yet Pip's so-called desire in the novel, is much more about indefatigable hopes built around his perceived deficiencies. A revolving door of shame about his common labouring self, his coarse hands and thick boots, that forever marks his inferiority; a lack explicitly announced to him on his first meeting with Estella and Miss Havisham. Pip's return to the realism that his old working-class existence can be reborn, or reconfigured in ways that enlarge his existence, resides in his acceptance of the goodness in Magwitch and Joe, and in his ability to witness Joe's happy union with Biddy. Their marriage at the end of the novel, is the last hope (wedlock with Biddy) that perishes for Pip. But his love and remorse generate sincere thankfulness on seeing them so full of joy. Pip realises he is grateful: 'I had never breathed this last baffled hope to Joe' (Dickens, 1996, p. 479).

Are wants that are fed by ego ideals, hopes or desires? And what indeed makes the difference? Lacan would argue that for a desire to be real it has to be reciprocal, and yet the kind of hopes circling in *Great Expectations*, the ideals that are a debasement of our-selves or others, aren't really that kind of authentic exchange. Hope, as Boris shows us is about a belief in eternal time, and nothing, or we should say no-one, conjures this up more vividly than Dickens's character Miss Havisham. She represents trauma, the stopping of time, but also some kind of hideous preservation of the past, that can't be reshaped into anything new:

> So unchanging was the dull old house, the yellowed light in the darkened room, the faded spectre in the chair by the dressing table glass, that I felt as though the stopping of the clocks had stopped Time in its mysterious place, and, while everything outside it grew older, it stood still.
>
> (Dickens, 1996, p. 125)

Whilst this is such a vivid description of psychical trauma, it's also an encapsulation of late capitalist culture. Miss Havisham's hopeless arrest of time is not the opposite to Pip's unflagging hopes but its accompaniment. Hope has a tendency to detach itself from reality, when that ability to bear what's in front of us is challenged. We can hope in the face of climate change, but what if that hope, separated as it is from any realistic remedy, just enables us to continue without change, in some nostalgic and petrified illusion? The royal coronation in Britain in 2023 offered such false hope; the monarchy can modify just enough. After all, King Charles is all for green. We can tolerate the most amazing discrepancy of privilege and wealth against so much dire poverty, and much like Dickens's worlds, it is hope that is foregrounded. A hope against hope, that the fleetingness of our lives will be halted. So much tragedy is a bedfellow to lethal illusions. We could argue that there is nothing really realistic about tragedy, which is maybe why Freud is so upbeat about the virtues of transience in his paper 'On Transience'.

In a walk with the melancholic poet Rilke, who bemoans the changing of the seasons, the passing of summer into winter, Freud regards his sad friend and observes that the poet's eternal wish for the loveliness of nature is mistaken. He disputes:

> The pessimistic poet's view that the transience of what is beautiful involves any loss of its worth. On the contrary, an increase! Transience value is scarcity value in time. Limitation in the possibility of an enjoyment raises the value of the enjoyment.
>
> (Freud, 1916, p. 303)

Failing to change the poet's mind, Freud considers that as transience is a foretaste of mourning, it is the rebellion against mourning that the poet clings onto. Where we love and then lose, we refuse to give up on the love object, despite available substitutes. And this is what makes mourning, and the poet's melancholy in the face of changing seasons such a 'great riddle'.

But here Freud is talking about the impossible hope that survives in melancholia, the refusal to mourn, that it seems is locked into the ways in which we deny reality. Melancholia as Miss Havisham's eternal hope, and Pip's greatest expectations, can't give up or give way, to the mourning and transience which is integral, arguably to our aliveness, our ability to accept anything new. Maybe Kafka's aphorism, 'there is plenty of hope – an infinite amount of hope – but not for us', means that hope will always exist, but we have, unlike the poet, to embrace life's transience. A melancholia of hope fails to accept time's passing, becoming a form of living death. This mausoleum of ego ideals entraps and estranges us from finding life or its renewal.

If Freud and Boris see hope as a destructive wish fulfilment that won't broker either transience or disappointment, the philosopher Ernst Bloch puts hope centre stage as a utopian vision of the future that we need to embrace, if we want to see change. Bloch was a Marxist and saw the rise of fascism in 1930s Germany as rooted as much in the problems of left-wing politics as in those of the right. For Bloch the left was far too negative and needed a hopeful agenda for change. Indeed, Bloch was interested in the appeal of fascism to the German people, citing how those communities left behind by technological change and modernisation held on to nostalgia for the past that was exploited by the Nazis. Such populist appeal can be seen today in the hope fostered by Boris Johnson's government in the lead up to Brexit. However, false the hopeful vote from the working-class red wall Tories was in 2016, it was ignited by how forgotten about and left behind certain working-class communities felt. Their nostalgia although fed by current Tory party ideology, could be addressed by more progressive agendas. Something, perhaps Keir Starmer and a broad coalition on the left in our country still needs to listen to. My postman once asked me at the time of the coronation of King Charles if I was excited about it. And I replied to say I wasn't (privately thinking, 'why on earth do you support an institution that is structurally instrumental in making your life worse?'). However, his rejoinder is pertinent for this discussion, he just laughed, saying, 'what else have we got to look forward to?'

Bloch's view was that the left had to offer up hope, some kind of optimism in the face of despair. The present moment for Bloch, much like for psychoanalysis is shadowed, and to an extent unknowable. In the everyday moment there is an excess of what he called the 'not yet conscious' which carries the seeds of a better future. We might not optimise or be aware of this potential, but it is always lying in wait for future realisation. The 'not yet conscious' of our becoming can be found in everyday dreams and fairy tales. They can be found in theatres and films, fashion and performance. He gives the example of how dressing up can help channel different parts of our personality, that have hitherto been submerged. 'With garments', Bloch writes, 'women in particular put on a new part of themselves ... the wish to try oneself out in various ways also begins for most other people with the both spotless and variable illusion which a tailor can lend' (Bloch, 1986, p. 341).

Hope for Bloch lies not so much in a fantasy, but in the meeting place between fantasy and reality. In other words, it's the illusion this meeting place heralds, the exchange between fantasy and reality that is mediated by our will and desire:

> More than once the fiction of the happy end, when it seized the will, when the will had learnt both through mistakes and in fact through hope as well, and when reality did not stand in too harsh contradiction to it, reformed a bit of the world, that is an initial fiction was made real.
>
> (Bloch, 1986, p. 443)

Is there a positive case to be made for hope? It seems hope can be childish, and poisonous; it can build up our shame, lead us astray, or keep us eternally preserved in some kind of endless refusal to develop, grow-up or change. But without it what is really possible?

Erik Erikson talks of a basic trust or hope that begins with the mother, and Winnicott elaborates on this to suggest that the good-enough mother is essential in providing that transitional meeting place between fantasy and reality – the meeting place of illusion. The transitional object starts for Winnicott between the baby and the mother. The breast begins as a magical (under omnipotent control) fantasy and is gradually mingled with an awareness of the real breast or mother that comes and goes. The transitional object is the meeting place where we both make-up and find the reality we can reside in. We never put the question to the baby, according to Winnicott, of 'Did you conceive of this or was it presented to you from without'. In other words, reality is an illusion that is both made up and found. This idea of a transitional object or illusion is similar to Bloch's idea of the fantasies and dreams of everyday living. The mother's one task, after helping her baby find illusion, Winnicott reminds us, is to slowly enable disillusionment. If this goes well the baby can move onto frustration and desire. Transitional phenomena the illusions and disillusions we encounter, not just as small children but all the way through life, are a paradox. Hope, as an illusion is part of that paradox, that needs transience and disillusion, to be part of something creative. Without these breaks and diminishments to slow down the Icarus nature of hope's flight, we are left with the omnipotence of time unlived, reality abandoned or untested. Such is the poisonous hope of Miss Havisham's.

For the Mandelstams, false hope abounds, there is hope, against hope, against hope. Nadezhda fails to save her husband, he is eventually tricked and murdered by Stalin in 1938, dying in a transit camp en-route to the gulag of Siberia. She does, however, preserve his poetry and in that rescue, in those poems, reside the transitional object of hope, the one lasting, true illusion along with her testament, of the terrors of Stalin's Russia.

Bloch's *Principles of Hope* can seem naively optimistic when compared say to the sharp melancholy of fellow Marxists like Adorno or Benjamin. And as I have mentioned the becoming Utopia of socialism is simply an impossibility with the impending doom of climate change. Nevertheless, like my postman acknowledged we arguably have to look forward, however undetermined our life might seem; otherwise, there is simply no point to anyone's future.

Pip's expectations at the end of Dickens's novel are slowly, but inexorably disillusioned, one after the other. The ending is an elegy to all Pip's lost hopes, but one final illusion comes into view. As Pip, returns to his old home, the forge, after many years abroad, he sees Joe in his familiar place at the kitchen fireside, and next to him a child sitting on Pip's old stool:

> and there, fenced into the corner with Joe's leg, and sitting on my own little stool looking at the fire, was – I again!
>
> 'We give him the name of Pip for your sake, dear old chap' said Joe ... ['W]e hoped he might grow a little bit like you, and we think he do.'
>
> (Dickens, 1996, p. 481)

In this repetition and reproduction of Pip's history with Joe's son, there is a difference. The becoming in a present moment, of Pip's potential, not for himself, but for the son of the man he loves. In this elegiac moment there is hope, but not for him, and perhaps this very transitional hope is something for all of us, that's worth having.

Hope as trust in another is an essential part of creative life, as Erikson points out:

> The absence of basic trust can best be studied in infantile schizophrenia, while lifelong underlying weakness of trust is apparent in adult personalities in whom withdrawal into schizoid and depressive states is habitual.
>
> (Erickson, 1995, p. 250)

Therapy is one place where trust over time can be re-established. For the psychoanalytic theorists who espouse only the poisonous nature of hope, there is a forgetting that all therapy, if it is going to work, embodies the illusion of the moment, unconscious seeds in the present, and of course the past, that can recapture and reimagine something new. The absence of hope and trust in the world we currently inhabit is everywhere; we are all living with increasing levels of madness. And yet for hope to flourish, for it to move and pass into nourishment, rather than toxicity, it has to find company. For there can be no hope that will feed us without mourning, no hope that can achieve anything without desire and reality. Above all there can be no eternal hope, for lived time depends on the transience of our hopes, our ability to relinquish them and re-find them again elsewhere. To face the practicality of what is in front of us, both individually and collectively, we need inspiration by a more paradoxical hope as a truly transitional phenomenon.

Notes

1 Cited in Mandelstam (1999, p. 13).
2 This quote came from a conversation between Kafka and his friend and biographer Max Brod, published as 'Der Dichter Franz Kafka' ('the poet Franz Kafka') in the literary journal *Die Neue Rundschau*.

References

Boris, H. N. (1994) *Envy*, Northvale, NJ, Jason Aronson.
Bloch, E. (1986) *The Principle of Hope*, volume 1, translated by N. Plaice, S. Plaice and P. Knight, Cambridge, MA, MIT Press.
Dickens, C. (1996) *Great Expectations*, London, Penguin.

Erikson, E. H. (1995) 'Eight Ages of Man', in *Childhood and Society*, London, Vintage Books.

Freud, S. (1912) On the Universal Tendency to Debasement in the Sphere of Love, in *The Standard Edition of the Complete Psychological Works of Sigmund Freud*, volume 11, translated by J. Strachey, London, Hogarth Press.

Freud, S. (1916) On Transience, in *The Standard Edition of the Complete Psychological Works of Sigmund Freud*, volume 14, translated by J. Strachey, London, Hogarth Press.

Freud, S. (1927) The Future of an Illusion, in *The Standard Edition of the Complete Psychological Works of Sigmund Freud*, volume 21, translated by J. Strachey, London, Hogarth Press.

Freud, S. (1929) Civilisation and Its Discontents, in *The Standard Edition of the Complete Psychological Works of Sigmund Freud*, volume 21, translated by J. Strachey, London, Hogarth Press.

Kaplan, R. D., Gray, J. and Thompson, H. (2023) The New Age of Tragedy, *The New Statesman*, 23 April.

Mandelstam, N. (1999) *Hope Against Hope: A Memoir*, translated from Russian by M. Hayward, London, Harvill Press.

2 The Shame Shell

Shame is perhaps the most pervasive and yet hidden feeling in our lives. Existing both everywhere and nowhere, shame is always a threat to our self and self-esteem, but it is also always a hide-out, some kind of secret, because of the pain it can inflict on ourselves and others. And as shame evolves in our life, it clandestinely shapes who we are and how we seem. Shame can make us hide and withdraw, it can make us shy and self-hating, but it is also to be found, lurking, behind the most persistent show-off. A master, often early on, in the arts of defence, shame is the signal of our dependence on others, it can be produced by our curiosity and sexuality, but in turn that very pleasure, our sexual enjoyment, can be the mask behind which our unlovable and alone shame-self dwells. Shame does not just shape the self; it becomes a shifter and operator in how society works and reproduces. If we feel pleasure, shame will lurk, threatening to spoil it. If we are successful, shame will tell us our pride is only a prelude to the fall. Where we dare to love shame will tell us we are unlovable. Where we are cruel, shame will tell us we enjoy it, and where we are hurt our shame tells us we deserve it. When we might show-off or boast, shame is waiting to remind of us our worthlessness. Shame is our shadow; it so often can also become our truth. Whenever, and wherever we see entitlement and privilege in the world; it is shored up by the shame and humiliation of those who are less deserving.

In Kazuo Ishiguro's novel *Klara and the Sun* we are introduced into the familiar bleak landscape (for Ishiguro) reminiscent of his earlier *Never Let Me Go*, where the world is divided by privilege and caste. Those who are gifted and therefore saved, and those who pay the price as servants to the anointed special individuals at the price of their own humanity. Servants being people seen as the class of humans who are less special but necessary through their bought labour or enslavement, to service the needs and designs of the rich. And of course, when people are placed in the lowest caste, they are not seen as human at all.

DOI: 10.4324/9781003515777-2

In *Never Let Me Go* the servants are the cloned children, raised in a boarding school like institution, who will grow up to provide the more 'human' population with replacement organs. It takes up to four operations for them to die or 'complete', the euphemism for the fulfilment of their role. In *Klara and the Sun*, the servants are robots, the Artificial Friends (AFs) who appear like mannequins in shop windows, and are bought to be playmates, nursemaids, friends for people's children. Klara is an AF bought for Josie by her mother. Josie is sick because she has been 'lifted', or genetically modified to make her more intelligent. Josie's sister has already died from being lifted, and as the novel progresses, we learn that Klara's role is to become a kind of clone to Josie; as a special sort of friend, she is to learn and imitate her gestures, voice, her manner of walking. Klara's role is to learn Josie's personality so intimately that she can continue Josie for her mother's benefit, in the sad event where Josie actually dies.

In one passage Josie's mother praises Klara for her perceptive ability to mimic Josie, but also offers more specific or strategic advice. 'That's right,' she says, asking her to move, 'Do something. Don't stop being Josie. Let me see you move a little.' Josie responds by settling into a lazy, drooping pose. That's great, the mother affirms, asking her to speak. And when Klara is unsure, the mother becomes insistent that she only wants Josie, Klara is now redundant and must disappear from view, continuing Josie by becoming her mind and body (Ishiguro, 2021, p. 104). Ishiguro's novels are about the ever-increasing lengths society will go to in self-preservation, and how this self-preservative drive accumulates entitlement and self-absorption for the lucky minority. He also demonstrates the organising shame that results with this increasing absorption in the self. In this scenario, shame accumulates in line with the privilege we award ourselves. Privilege is never stable there is always someone that is cleverer, wealthier, happier and more beautiful than you. Consequently, the shame that this recognition can provoke, can be too painful to consider and so it becomes projected onto those we consider less worthy of humanity, or care.

What Ishiguro is describing among other things is the coupling of narcissism and shame that accompanies the rampant individuality in contemporary culture. The violence that ensues when we put the narcissism of our ego ideals ahead, and in front, of our love and our communal fellowship with each other.

I want to discuss some of Freud's ideas in relation to our sense of shame in today's society. But why is Freud pertinent and what makes him worth taking note of rather than other ideas on shame that might be more contemporary? Well, first, shame in Freud's work is everywhere and nowhere. Although he didn't write explicit papers on shame, Freud understood that we repress what feels and what is experienced as too much. Whether that is our libidinal needs, our sexual desires, our rage and so forth. The power of shame comes in its privacy, and he became especially interested in the ways that shame comes to haunt the ways in which we see and experience ourselves as replete individuals in the lives we lead. There is the ego or person that adapts to the world and there is the shadow or shame that marks that ego, inadequate or sham. In 1914 Freud introduced his paper 'On Narcissism', which disrupted his libidinal drive theory that had hitherto been the main meat of psychoanalytic thinking. Where before Freud's thinking on shame had been focused on shame as either an affectual force, or a guard against that disturbing affect. In 'On Narcissism' Freud introduces shame as a conflict within the self, an intrapsychic conflict. Intrinsic to this famous paper is Freud's concept of the ego-ideal where the individual 'has set up an ideal in himself by which he measures his actual (self)'. The development of the ego ideal corresponds to the gradual internalisation of a narcissistic object:

> The subject's narcissism makes its appearance displaced onto this new ideal(self), which like the infant's self, finds itself possessed of every perfection that is of value ... what he projects before him as his ideal is the substitute for the lost narcissism of his childhood in which he was his own ideal ...
>
> (Freud, 1914, p. 94)

Here, shame is the recovery, projected onto our preferred ego ideals of the perfect self-love we experienced as children. Except with primary narcissism there is no criticism. Babies don't judge themselves. They are not split as adults are into the part of the self that censors and the suffering supplicant ... the other part of us that can never attain that perceived ideal self. When we are infants, the ego ideal is simply an admixture of love for the mother, and love of the self. Indeed, it is a part of this primary narcissism that positive identification with, and energy towards, the mother transfers to the ideal, thus making the child more independent of the adult. As Annie Reich suggests the early ego ideal allows the child 'to become more independent of the love, praise, and encouragement of his objects, attempting to avoid disappointment and frustration by living up to his ideal self' (Reich, 1960, p. 220). Yet, we can also see how striving to be an ideal self can fill ourselves with shame about our bodily and libidinal needs. And so, it follows, that the later division that Freud describes between the ideal ego and the self can also easily be perceived as becoming part of the defence against frustration and need for another.

In their paper 'The Ego Ideal and the Ideal Self', Sander, Holder and Meers make a distinction between shame in relation to an ego ideal and the guilt we experience in the face of our critical self-judgement. In shame we lose in comparison to the person we want to be. We also fail in comparison to how we want to be perceived or seen by others. In guilt, however, the self says to itself 'I do not really want to be what I feel I ought to be'. In guilt we fall short of who we ought to be in accordance with the jurisdiction of the Super-ego, the rules of originally our parents and society (Sander et al., 1963, p. 157). As Adam Phillips notes, there is an ambivalent protest in guilt, about the rules, that we might repress, but also leaves us a get-out, the possibility of rebellion that can keep us going on either side of the moral question, so to speak.

Whereas in shame there is no such doubt, we are all essentialists, 'when we are ashamed of ourselves we know what we have done and we know that it is terrible; it was already known to be terrible' (Phillips, 2019, p. 43). And this is what makes shame, for Phillips, so irreducible: we can't interpret, or read or move it in any sufficient way. Because of this it's hard to talk about shame either inside the therapy room or outside in terms of everyday life. Perhaps the easiest thing is to just pass it on, which is so often why we need the perceived servants and workers to enact our shame for us. When we feel shame, it becomes a feeling we can't really bear to have, or really face, and so our unbearable encounter with shame is passed onto someone who is convenient to despise and disgrace. Shame is a story that is so easy to pass on, and the people we like to shame, are all too often the ones that remind us of our own weakness, our envy, and our past humiliations.

Klara is the robot and the recipient in Ishiguro's novel of everybody's desires and needs and at times their shame. She magically moulds herself into doing and being what everybody wants. And the most remarkable and liberating thing about Klara is that she herself has no shame – she is a robot. Thus, she readily embodies for everyone in the novel, and for us as readers, not just the Sun, but what could be called, not so much a best self, but our most alive sensibility. Although Klara is a non-human machine, she is also the character that perhaps conjures up most, desire; a pure and rather impersonal flame or force like the Sun that passes through her and beyond her. Klara's purpose to help, principally Josie, but also all the people that love Josie, is not besieged by vicious mantras of impossible perfections. Klara might be a servant or helper, but she is also the heroine of the novel. Her impersonality as a robot whose desire is to help others is simple. With no moral virtue, or exchange value attached, Klara's desire is something that saves her from the various masochistic defences enacted by the other servants in Ishiguro's previous novels. Stevens, the servant in *The Remains of the Day*, idealises and is in awe of his upper-class employer, refusing to see his master's obvious fascist affiliations and tendencies. Whereas, in *Never Let Me Go*, Kathy and the other cloned children cope with their hideous fate through complex disavowals of what exactly their guardian's plans have in store for them.

Klara, on the other hand, has a clear purpose and desire to help Josie. She has exceptional observational powers for a robot, and she is particularly perceptive of the mother and daughter's relationship in the house where they all live. When Mother, who is constantly covering her negative emotions and shame, admits her envy to Klara, she tells her straight that she envies Klara's ability to have no feelings. But after contemplation, Klara remarks that she has many feelings and the more she observes herself, the more feelings she sees, and the more feelings are at her disposal (Ishiguro, 2021, pp. 97–98). Klara's sight of other people and the world comes in squares and boxes. Like a computer she records the mother's emotions in one box, the mother's smiling lips and cruel humour, in another sadness, and yet in another real kindness. However, the mother is trapped in the ego ideal of what she wants her daughter to be. Guilty at the damage she has caused her daughter by having her 'lifted', the mother is ambivalent. And yet she can't give up the artistic and intellectual ambitions she has for her daughter. These ego ideals coalesce into the mother plotting with the AF designer Mr Capaldi to make Klara into a continuation of Josie, a living doll who excels in human performance, so that her mother will not lose Jodie when she dies. Like the ultimate commodity fetish or object, Klara is in fact everybody's ego ideal, especially the mother's ideal for her daughter.

In 'On Narcissism' Freud reminds us of how parental love is just the resurrection of the parent's infantile narcissism projected onto their children. Surely, parental love must amount to more than just a rebirth of our original complete (in our eyes) selves projected onto our kids? For parenting to be more than this, parents have to love their children aside from their ideals of them. Something, that is not as easy to separate out as we may think. It's easy enough to love our children but it's a whole lot more difficult to love our children for how they uniquely are. To see them in all their unknowable differences and so back their desire. When the mother brings Klara to Mr Capaldi to see if she will fit into an AF that will be Josie, she tries to explain to Klara what she has in mind. Telling Klara she is remarkable, the mother explains that after Sal, Josie's older sister, was lifted, and didn't make it, the father didn't want to risk doing the same thing to Josie. Making clear she is not blaming Paul, Josie's father, because his feelings after his elder daughter's death are understandable, the mother makes it clear that she could never envisage an 'unlifted' life for Josie. Lots of children don't become lifted, but the mother wanted the best for her remaining daughter, her best life. And now Josie is sick, because of what she, the mother had chosen. Appealing to Klara, the mother asks her self-pityingly to consider how hard her choice has been (Ishiguro, 2021, p. 213).

The mother's calculation might seem chilling, but how different is it really from the direction and distraction of so much middle-class parenting today, where children's abilities and education have to be optimised at the earliest opportunity. The lure of giving children a good life means more and more pressure on kids from schools and families to achieve. We might not have genetically engineered intelligent, children; but we increasingly divide our kids into those that are paid for by private education and are expected to do well, and their 'unlifted' counterparts in the state sector. Winnicott's wise understanding of how children need to learn the 'capacity to be alone' means parents have to leave their kids be, that is to say not to abandon them but to allow them free reign to idle, to be left to their own devices. For Winnicott, the capacity to be alone is a paradox, in that it is based on 'the experience of being alone in the presence of someone' (for Winnicott this initial someone is the mother). This ability to be alone with someone else is also, in Winnicott's view, the basis for ordinary friendship:

> Now, if I am right in the matter of the paradox, it is interesting to examine the nature of the relationship to the infant to the mother, that which for the purposes of this paper I have called ego-relatedness. It will be seen I attach a great importance to this relationship, as I consider that is the stuff out of which friendship is made. It may turn out to be the *matrix* of the transference.
>
> (Winnicott, 1982, p. 33)

Winnicott describes a much more friendly relationship within analysis, than has been traditionally reconstructed. For me, it rings true. If you can't be 'friends' with your client or patient then something becomes lost. This is not identical to friendship in everyday life, but it is not totally different either. The capacity to be alone in therapy is not nurtured by omnipotent interpretation as in some Kleinian varieties of psychoanalysis, but neither is it augmented by being a sort of neutral mute, as strict Lacanian approaches advocate. One of the qualities that Klara brings to her friendship role with Josie is precisely that friendship which in turn provides Josie with the 'capacity to be alone'; a capacity which has hitherto been jettisoned in the mother's anxious and preoccupied love for her daughter.

We seem, at the present time, in the way society is currently organised, to have completely lost that ability to leave children the freedom not to just discover their worlds but to create them with their own minds and imagination. Children need to develop ideals, internal and psychological values, that are arguably free to roam and discover. If accompanied and left alone in the right way, children will naturally develop these values. Prescriptive ideals, whether they come out of the mouths of parents or schools, produce kids who feel overwhelmed by the pressure to compete. Thus, shame emerges as the inevitable accompaniment to this ego race to be the fittest. Maybe within its history, childhood has always been filled with the humiliation the child experiences through failing to conform to adult expectations. But perhaps what has become more prevalent is the urge to mentally diagnose or pathologise those children that refuse to fit in with regimes of school or home life. With parents who are often juggling impossible demands of work and childrearing, having a naughty and disobedient child is rarely seen as an accomplishment. And maybe it should, in the sense that there is often so much creativity in the non-compliant child, whatever the deprivation. Trying to coerce a disruptive child into being good, whether we use bribes or the 'naughty step', is often at the risk of not acknowledging the communication of that young person's 'true' self.

In *Klara and the Sun*, the mother observation of her daughter is categorically different from her 'artificial' friend. Klara's observation of Josie is based on an intuitive perception of what she needs, but the mother's gaze is a constant measurement of Josie as to her talents and virtues; a gaze which Josie finds both intrusive and embarrassing. Commenting on her daughter's artwork one day, the mother tells Josie that although she really likes her daughter's black and white sketches, she bemoans that Josie has seemingly 'given up' on her colour pencils. The mother misses her daughter's colour pictures. Josie replies that her colour pictures are a major source of awkwardness and embarrassment. Having none of this, the mother insists that these painterly pictures are beautiful to behold and leave people with wonder. To shut her up, Josie remarks that all parents think that their kid's creations are amazing, because of the evolutionary process. It is at this point that the mother steps up her manipulation, suddenly suggesting that the whole conversation is linked to a recent meeting where a neighbour's child made a sarcastic remark about a poster Josie had made. Reminding her daughter of a situation where her artwork has been envied in the past and is now happening again, she remarks, 'That young lady was jealous of your talent'. It's not the neighbour's child's jealousy that disturbs Josie, but her mother's narcissistic attachment that spouts envy when Josie begins to assert her difference (Ishiguro, 2021, p. 51).

Josie points out that her colour pictures are as bad as her mother's cello playing. And yet the mother insists that whilst her cello playing sounds like the grandmother of Dracula, Josie's use of colour is more like a beautiful garden pool on a summer evening. Mothers often narcissistically invest in their children's talents as a means to protect them from the perceived failures and traumas of that mother's own personal history. Josie's only rejoinder to her mum's insistence to be excellent and enviable in something she might not want, or doesn't feel up to achieving, is to throw the whole problem back to her, saying she will consider going back to her colour pictures, only if her mother resumes her terrible cello playing. What would it mean for us as individuals and as a society to start freeing ourselves from the ego ideals that keep us too captured? So many best or preferred selves, places to go, houses to own, children to optimise, people to be? The vicious irony of anybody's ego ideal is that it's a fantasy. Even if we think we achieve these ideals, they can't nourish us because they are a self-circuit back to an impossible narcissism that we can only resurrect through a projection that will never yield the happiness we strive for. Ego ideals when they are too fixed or pursued too relentlessly produce a shame that is ubiquitous and fundamental, because we Will fail them and the punishment they exact is as cruel as it is repetitive and monotonous. There is nothing surprising about this sadomasochistic bond that goes round and round like a merry go round and leads nowhere. Young people turn up to therapy all the time telling me they just want to be their best self. That their unhappiness would somehow disappear, if they could stop being failures and be attractive, because they are ugly, smart where they feel stupid, unkind and bad because they have difficult feelings about their friends and so on. What is astonishing in these young people is how warped and completely condemning the judgments about themselves actually are. How completely at odds these self-criticisms seem to be with who these young people are in their true selves. I respond by encouraging these newly adults, to be experimental and to take risks. We also talk about their inevitable anger with their parents and their need to leave home. A lot of young people feel tremendous guilt at the conflicts they feel about their families, most especially if those homes have been loving ones. One of the biggest hurdles is to persuade these incredibly likeable young people, to forget about themselves and the endless shopping list of their flaws. To stop measuring themselves obsessively against their preferred self – be beautiful, clever, successful or whatever is their latest complaint on how they don't make the grade. We all haul our preferred selves around with us as literally the burden on our backs. Bowing us all in shame and servitude to an 'idée fixe', an ideal that at its most extreme terrorises all of us. We are all bullies to our masochistic egos, often, especially when we are trying our hardest to improve ourselves. Self-improvement can perhaps never be a therapeutic ideal that yields growth or change.

In *Mourning and Melancholia* Freud describes a similar splitting in the ego as the one that happens in shame between the ideal ego and the self. But here he is talking about the ambivalent relation to the lost object experienced through grief. Unlike mourning where the lost object can be a radical undoing of the ego, a loss that leads to desire, in melancholia the ego retreats. Withdrawing her ego from its desiring ties with the world, the melancholic identifies instead with the lost object: 'Thus the shadow of the object fell upon the ego, and the latter can be judged by a special agency, as though it were an object, the forsaken object' (Freud, 1917, p. 249).

Freud notices that the melancholic complaints although self-accusatory are not really vicious assaults on the self. They are more like old-fashioned 'plaints' from litigants who put forward a legal plea for restitution or justice. The guilt of the melancholic proceed from a huge 'constellation of revolt', an ambivalence and rage against the lost object that has taken up residence inside the self. Here, we can see, how much hatred and resentment of the other inhabits this form of guilt, a rebellion over what should never have been taken away, never lost. 'Self-reproaches are reproaches against a loved object which have been shifted away from it onto the patient's own ego' (Freud, 1917, p. 248).

In guilt we feel bad about letting down someone else. But in shame we betray ourselves unequivocally. Thus, in shame, there is no cover for, or ambiguity about our sins. No court of Law, or judge and jury to decide. We are always cast down.

In fact, although shame historically has been seen as primarily a social phenomenon, as proceeding from the objectification by the Other's gaze. Shame might also be seen as the ultimate in a private expression of self-hate. Sartre bases his whole argument of self-consciousness, what he calls 'consciousness at a keyhole' on the experience of shame. What he describes is a man looking through a keyhole listening and looking. And then the man becomes aware of footsteps in the hall and realises that someone is looking at him. The man's objectification in that gaze, is the condition of his social subjectivity and self. No objectification or shame means no personal identity. As Sartre reasons, shame 'is the recognition of the fact that I am indeed that object which the Other is looking at and judging' (Sartre, 1966, p. 350).

Aristotle also understands shame in relation to our social position via other people. Shame arises when we feel shunned by a community or person we wish to be accepted or associated with, and abjection results:

Since Shame is the imagination of disgrace, in which we shrink from the disgrace itself and not from its consequences, and we only care what opinion is held of us because of the people who form that opinion, it follows that the people before which we feel shame are those whose opinion of us matters to us.

(Aristotle, 1985 pp. 114–115)

Shame for Aristotle occurs in relation to people who 'admire us, those whom we admire, those by whom we wish to be admired'.

And yet if shame is the condition of our sociability, it is also our failure, the refusal by me or another, of our acceptability into fellowship and shared feeling. Freud always confused his ideas of the ego ideal and the superego, mixing them up or choosing one or another term in his various essays. If in his paper 'On Narcissism' the ego ideal is clearly our lost narcissistic object projected onto a preferred self. In *Mourning and Melancholia* the superego is a critical conscience making us guilty, albeit an agency as Freud points out we are only ambivalently tied to. Thus, the ego ideal is the person we love and admire, whereas the superego is a law we can secretly ignore or get around. It seems that shame elicits the most self-hate because it comes from the place of most self-love. And so, it's interesting to ask why is it so difficult to return from shame to a more loving relationship to ourselves and fellowship with others?

When a woman is raped, her shame is linked to her absolute powerless. The rapist objectifies and obliterates her – rape is the ultimate act of control and objectification. The rape act speaks ultimate power lessness and control over a woman and her body. It's as if the rapist says to his victim, 'I hate you and can obliterate you, meanwhile you are precisely nothing. I exist whereas you don't exist for anything but degradation.' We could argue that the virulence of the shame that raped women are left with is social. The law, police, courts, often continue that shaming or making the woman feel that is she who somehow is a disgrace, rather than the man responsible. And yet when you work with that shame clinically it is clear that the worst crime of the rapist is that he robs the woman of her more private self-esteem, her complete ability to love herself, to feel beautiful and to desire again. This is a much deeper wound that a shame that is conveyed by social groups or institutions, although they remain a mirror to the savage judgment the woman can enact on herself. And yet women do recover from rape, although there is always a price, a cost for their resilience.

Do rapists ever feel shame about the women they violate? Does Harvey Weinstein, now, locked up for his crimes, feel shame? I have no idea. My suspicion is that his shame has all been displaced onto the women he very much hates. Weinstein is more likely to just feel self-pity, the other thin-skinned, sensitive side to his rage; his original self-cure for whatever slights, real or imagined, he has suffered at the hands of a first woman. Often, in shameless cultures and clubs of, say, misogynist men, the shame is displaced and passed onto women. But why? And why is it so accepted and normalised that mothers are always unforgiven and guilty for the rage of their sons, or that women have to take on the repair of that rage; or pay a sacrificial forfeit with their lives and bodies? In a widely publicised rape trial in France in 2024, a woman was drugged by Dominique Pelicot, a supposed loving husband, by crushing pills into her evening meal. The husband then raped and filmed the abuse of his wife, when she was unconscious, and invited a local community of men to also take part, over a series of years. The woman who waived her right to anonymity, Gisèle Pelicot, changed her status from victim to heroine overnight by making the trial and the men who attacked her open to public scrutiny. Her now-famous words to the thousands of women in France that flocked to the trial in her defence were 'it's not for us to feel shame, it's them'. The tremendous courage of this woman has highlighted how the shame for rape is constantly reverberating onto the victims because the men, and the patriarchy responsible, don't feel the shame they should. Whatever fantasies these men were entertaining when they abused this woman, the entitlement and misogyny, not just of these men individually but of the everyday culture, is there for all of us to see. The case has universally shocked and repulsed people, and yet it shows how shame operates on both a social and private level. Without the public exposure of this case, because of one woman's heroic actions, the shame of this sexual violence would of assumed its familiar silent passage from abuser to victim travelling unnoticed as it fuelled the misogyny that originally created the crime.

What would it take, what would have to happen for shame not to be passed on as it is in our contemporary world? Passed on, more often, by cultures or tribes that feel an entitlement to be superior, even if that inherent deserving is questionable. But like my imagined self-pity of Harvey Weinstein, men who routinely hate women enough to harm them are shameless about their hate. Such men don't exist behind some kind of shame barrier or threshold. It's not the case, as they might like you to think, that they are really shame free. Many men's misogyny is rooted in envy and the original wound for them is always some perceived loss, rejection or inadequacy they were made to feel at the hands of their individual mothers. And let's not forget mothers are always already guilty, and so eternally deserving of punishment. Motherhood is the terrain, to quote Adrienne Rich, that not just patriarchy, but also the normalisation of envying women is erected.

Passing on shame is done in shameless cultures, where it looks as if the shame has disappeared, when in fact what is being enacted is a kind of revenge. Because however strong the so-called shameless person feels, whatever omnipotence and entitlement he has sought to cloak his weakness with.; the shame remains as a stain or narcissistic slight that goes back a very long way, probably to childhood. Shamelessness can be catching. Cultures of shamelessness, like the various recent Tory governments in Britain, make shamelessness into a veritable badge of honour, if not pride. Boris Johnson was lauded for his shamelessness, it was part of his appeal to the Tory rank and file, because he seemed to be saying, 'You can be like me, where the rules don't apply. We might be the government and responsible for people's safety and well-being, but we don't have to take these roles too seriously. We can party, whilst other people are in lockdown or dying from COVID, because we don't really value being compassionate about the poor and the sick and the disabled in our society.'

Indeed, respect or kindness for those less fortunate than themselves becomes, if anything, something to be despised by these government ministers because it connotes an understanding of the vulnerability in people. The horror of this vulnerability is what then must be stamped out and disavowed by so many of our unelected authorities. Whatever the original shame these Tory ministers might have felt, there shame becomes washed away in a reverse value system. What is shameful it seems is to be poor, or resourceless. To be stateless or homeless is unforgivable. As in Ishiguro's dystopian worlds, the governing elites or establishments in British life seem to wilfully ignore or actively punish those whom by their very lack of power are seen as some kind of contaminating threat. Any violent punishment or inhumanity, it seems, is entirely justified if you are a migrant or a beggar. It is the beggar in *Klara and the Sun* who Klara notices as the first person to receive the Sun's nourishment. At first, Klara assumes the beggar and his dog have died because instead of standing and interacting with people passing by they are lying down on the pavement. But then she realises she has been mistaken. Klara looks at the place on the pavement where she had presumed the beggar and his dog died, only to realise they actually weren't dead after all. The sun had sent an exceptional nourishment to save them. The beggar was even beginning to stir and sit up. And in time, later in the day, he would perhaps be on his feet chatting away to the people passing the doorway in his characteristic way (Ishiguro, 2021, p. 37).

Shame in shameless cultures must be avoided at all costs. In his seminal work *The Making of Them: The British Attitude to Children and the Boarding School System*, Nick Duffy spells out, how boarding schools in Britain have operated historically to forge officers and gentle-man fit to govern and rule in the name of empire and nation. These educational establishments have also been a way to cross the class divide, as the nouveau rich gain aspirational advantage by sending their children to such schools. However, the aim of boarding schools is also to stamp out vulnerability, emotion and all the helplessness associated with childhood. These children are effectively orphaned when they are sent away to school, in the sense that dependency on parents, especially the mother, is irrevocably ruptured. Thus, boarding school becomes for many children a systematic form of abuse that can be very hard to recover from:

> The British boarding school system is an anachronism bogged down in its colonial past. It became popular due to the parent's desire for status, which it has served handsomely. It is underpinned be a negative attitude to children, which I shall argue also applies to women, foreigners, and what counsellors call the 'Child Within'. Boarding Schools will remain popular as long as the two-nation class system remains in place, because it is an instrument which guarantees its continuation. It therefore splits the nation in two, as it does intrapsychically, its pupils.
>
> (Duffy, 2000, p. 13)

'Boarding school syndrome', as it is now called, is the acknowledgement, at least with survivors and the therapeutic communities who seek to help them, of the humiliation, childhood abuse (emotional, physical and sexual) and lasting shame that induction into upper-class existence can involve. But boarding school doesn't just shame young school pupils, it also teaches them that in order to survive, they have cut off their feel-ings, their needs and all sense of their vulnerability. Unfortunately, this also entails for many children learning to bully and dominate the kids that are younger or perceived as weaker. Becoming an upper-class gen-tleman is about being courageous, and masterful; it is about winning and being spirited. So, shame gets passed down a line of privilege. It is easy perhaps to see how boarding schools perpetuate shameless cultures of mostly white, male entitlement, where accumulation of wealth and suc-cess for these individuals becomes a route, or a way, they can distance themselves from 'ordinary' people's suffering. There are winners and losers. The disadvantaged are to be pitied at best, and at worst feared as a threat. This repugnance aimed often at the most vulnerable in society, is also a defence against the cycles of humiliation and shame that are perpetuated in 'growing' so many of the leaders of modern Britain.

Shame is not simply something that is passed around in class culture. Like trauma, shame is a seed which branches and blossoms into more shame, with each subsequent encounter until it becomes a large inside tree. A tree which becomes continually fed by the fury of punishing ego ideals. Shame is seemingly a sadomasochistic and unconscious pact, often within the self, that one is dirty or unclean, or abject. Whilst the other is superior, clean and of course an unassailable judge. As Mary Douglas in her book *Purity and Danger* has shown, the discrimination of what is abject is socially and historically contextualised. But that doesn't stop our shame being the cruel arbitrator within the internal theatre of ourselves.

In Annie Ernaux's memoir *Shame*, she relives the powerful event that instigated her lifelong acquaintance with mortification. The powerful first or primal scene occurred in the summer of Ernaux's 12th year, the year of her communion. Annie's parents were shopkeepers and one afternoon her domineering mother started arguing with her father, not stopping for the duration of their meal. The father says nothing, until eventually he rises shaking, dragging his wife into the neighbouring cellar where he grabs a scythe, at the same time holding Annie's mother 'by the shoulders or maybe the neck' (Ernaux, 2023, p. 13). Then it is over, and they are all back in the kitchen. Amidst all the sobbing, Annie remembers saying to her father, 'You'll breathe disaster on me'. From then on Annie is traumatised and vigilant. She has to stop her father killing her mum, to prevent him going to prison. Everyday small talk or gestures between her parents, every embrace, is only a pause before the catastrophe occurs. Her communion year spells the break between child and adulthood, between innocence and acute self-consciousness. Because Annie is traumatised, a veil descends separating her from the world, everything is unreal. 'I would behave normally but somehow I wasn't there'. Sent to a private convent school, the only child in her extended family to go, Annie excels in her studies and internalises her teacher Mademoiselle as an adored role model. From now on everything is measured between what is good and clean and what is abject and impure. Annie becomes acutely aware of the public discourse of the shop-keepers community, the politeness versus the private coarser family manners. She is always seeing herself and her family with a shameful filled measurement. The class difference that marks the difference between her aspiring private school and her family's more modest circumstances. Being dropped off one evening by Mademoiselle and other girls at her home, a dishevelled and sleepy mother comes to the door. Her nightgown is 'Both creased and soiled (we would use the garment to wipe ourselves after peeing)' (Ernaux, 2023, p. 72). Mademoiselle and the girls are struck silent. Annie rushes into the house to close the embarrassment down. In her memory she writes:

This scene, although barely comparable to the one in which my father tried to kill my mother, is its sequel. As if the sight of my mother's loose, unsupported flesh and her suspect nightgown had exposed the life we lived and who we truly were.

(Ernaux, 2023, p. 72)

Shame follows shame and beckons it into being. Cruelty settles in society's markers of who fits and who is out of place, and yet the cruelty that shame inflicts on us is perhaps inescapable. The identification of what we want and who we want to be can so easily be turned into a total attack of who we are. So how can we have ideals without self-hate? How can we free our dreams of self-accomplishment from the accompanying cruelty of shame that seems to track them? What's the hope? It's an interesting question.

In *Klara and the Sun*, hope seems to visit everyone, even Klara. Whether it's the mother's rather poisonous wish to have lifted children, or Mr Capaldi's equally suspect desire of making Klara into an invention to continue Josie; or even the more alive hope of Josie's family and friends that she will recover. There is hope too, for the artificial friend Klara, who persuades Josie's father Paul to hunt down the awful Cootings Machine, a metaphor for the human destruction of our climate. Destroying this machine and stopping its pollution and fumes, Klara believes, will save Josie. Hope, it seems, like shame, is everywhere, whether it's the company our furious ego-ideals keep, or whether it's sprung in freedom away from them. Hope is, as Paul reminds Klara, that 'damn thing that never leaves you alone' (Ishiguro, 2021, p. 222).

Towards the end of *Klara and the Sun*, when Josie is very sick. The fear is that she is dying. The mother, unable to contemplate or bear the pain she is feeling, starts to berate Josie's friend Rick, who has always been trusted and true. Confronting Rick, the mother asks him whether or not he feels a winner in the game of chance with her life, Josie has played. The mother admits she shook the dice for her daughter, but it was always going to be Josie, not her that won or lost (Ishiguro, 2021, p. 280). The mother accuses Rick, Josie's unlifted friend, of playing it safe. Cruelly jibing him, she asks exactly what does he feel he has achieved or won? Gesturing to the window, she tells him to consider his future; he has played for the lowest stakes. And whatever he wins will be paltry and meagre. He might feel pleased with himself, but she was here to remind him, he had no right to feel that way. Unable to stand her guilt and shame at her decision to have her daughter 'lifted', the mother attacks Rick. He might be going to live but he would never attain the future she had envisaged for her daughter, a tomorrow, 'worthy of her spirit'. Not being able to accept her own shame at the competition she has made her daughter play, the mother's narcissistic investment in her daughter having a brilliant future has been at the cost of Josie's health and it seems her life. And so of course, the mother passes that shame on to Rick, Josie's loyal friend, humiliating him for his lower-class status as 'unlifted'.

If the answer to moving our shame is fundamentally about our ability to love and desire again then we have to distinguish between a shame that can be understood in terms of our desire – something that can transfigured. And a shame that is always stuck in relation to an excoriating ego ideal, like the mother's; one that has to arguably be abandoned because it is a closed circuit. With the latter, shame cannot be moved it just gets bigger with every circle of self-measurement and competitive scrutiny. Even if we can acknowledge how destructive and insular this shaming of the self becomes. It is perhaps harder to perceive how it acts as a guard or shield to another form of shame, the kind of shame that Freud realised was operative in terms of our desire. Perhaps, we have to abandon the shame in feeling we have failed ourselves, so we can experience a moveable shame in the helpless need of our desires? Desires in all their myriad force.

Within Ishiguro's novels, shame is the secret carried by privilege. In these worlds, the shame that is disavowed by the superior beings, lands on the unfortunates that are exploited to work for them. Stevens, the butler in *The Remains of the Day*, realises eventually the masochistic waste his life has been serving his master: 'I gave my best to Lord Darlington. I gave him the very best I had to give and now – well – I find I do not have a great deal more left to give' (Ishiguro, 1989, p. 242).

What makes Klara so different is that as a machine she can't be objectified or degraded in any shameful way. She is, as the mother comments, made of simply 'fabric'. When Miss Helen, the mother of Rick, meets Klara for the first time, she remarks on the difficulty in knowing how to behave in relation to the non-human Klara: 'After all are you a guest at all? Or do I treat you like a vacuum cleaner?' (Ishiguro, 2021, p. 145).

Because Klara is a literal object, she can't be humiliated or degraded. In fact, her purpose to help in a completely non-sacrificial way turns her desire, like the sun, into a literal life force, something that augments the other characters love for Josie and their wish for her to get better. Finally, it is the Sun, called upon by Klara and pouring through the window, that bathes Josie in his rays … As the sun lights up Josie and her bed in a burning halo of orange, the mother standing nearest has to shield her face. Rick, the friend, perhaps understandably grasps that, like the beggar man, Josie is being restored and saved by the glorious sun.

And yet as Klara looks on she can see how the mother, together with the housekeeper Melania, have also grasped the truth of what is happening with the sun's rays (Ishiguro, 2021, p. 284).

Perhaps there is no better description of what unconscious desire can really be than this depiction of Klara as a non-personal life or solar force. A power that does not so much inhabit people, as in some kind of secret or hidden container. Rather, this non-personal desire passes through people; a force that can visit them but also exists outside them, beyond the boundaries of their personal self.

In Freud's early writings *Studies on Hysteria*, which he wrote with Breuer, he writes of how his work is to override a 'psychical force in the patients which was opposed to the pathogenic ideas becoming conscious (being remembered)':

> From these I recognised the universal characteristics of such ideas. They were all of a distressing nature, calculated to arouse the affects of shame, of self-reproach and of psychical pain and the feeling of being harmed, they were all of a kind that one would prefer not to have experienced, that one would rather forget.
>
> (Breuer and Freud, 1895, pp. 268–269)

From this Freud moves onto his ideas of defence, and so to his seminal idea of repression, the repelling of the offending idea by the ego so it can be rendered innocuous or harmless. In his early case work with the famous Dora, Freud realises that clinically shame does not even have to be unconscious it is just kept secret:

> In the first place, patients consciously and intentionally keep back part of what they ought to tell – things that are perfectly well known to them – because they have not got over their feelings of timidity and shame.
>
> (Freud, 1905, p. 17)

Thus shame, for Freud, is both a repressed unconscious affect, and a more conscious defence against hidden desire. Shame in a clinical context is a beast or hydra with many heads. It is always waiting in the wings of the clinical encounter. If spoken about too soon or too insensitively it erupts and blossoms in all kinds of negative unspeakable ways which can often terminate the therapy. Shame can't be ignored, but often it has to be sensed rather than directly spoken about. As the underbelly of the transference shame shows up as a symptom or feeling that needs elaborating. Or shame emerges as a defence against desire and relatedness;

in the mental torsions, we could even call them the perversions of a punishing ego ideal. Shame it seems, is never equal, there are many shames, and some need more attention paying to them than others. For example, acknowledging the shame and fear, many men feel about their misogyny and hatred of women, can be worthwhile. Especially because so many of these men are heterosexual, where they feel shame, they also need and desire. Besides, women, overall, prefer men who are able to really like them as people, not just lust after them as a basic nutrient.

At the end of *Klara and the Sun*, Klara is left to fade out in the Yard, and her old store manager passes by. The manager asks Klara how her work experience with Josie's family has been. She reminisces about the day the mother and Josie came in to choose and buy Klara. She remembers especially the mother's test to Klara, making and watching her walk. The manager admits she had been worried on Klara's behalf. Klara answers by saying she would never have attained 'accuracy' in continuing Josie. Mr Capaldi had not believed there was anything unique to Josie that could not be replicated or continued in Klara. He had searched in vain for a special something but there was nothing that could not be reproduced. Klara declares that Mr Capaldi could never have succeeded because he was looking in the wrong place. That exceptional thing wasn't to be found in Josie, instead it lived on inside those who loved her. Thus, Klara could never have continued Josie, which is why she was glad she had decided as she did.

Shame is like as shell or carapace in which we hide away from what we need, and what is waiting outside of ourselves. Inside the shell, it feels very painful, but it's a peculiarly addictive form of pain, because however much it depletes and savages us, we remain safe from any perceived threat to the ever-increasing fragility of our identity and selves. Escaping this shell, crawling out into the sunlight, even at a snail's pace, is really not dependant on more self-conscious evaluations of our identity. Identity politics might seem to herald a righteous assertion of how selves, that have hitherto been marginalised, can now be championed. But like Sartre's self-awareness at the keyhole, the popular attention to our identities, the scrutiny of what constitutes our gendered, sexual and racialised selves can lead in counter-productive ways to the most enormous competition. In this game selves are measured and compared, slights are spotlighted and counted. The offence taken provides us with self-knowledge and subjectivity at the risk of permanent residency inside a shame shell. In contrast, the place we need to look is not inside ourselves; like Josie, there is nothing special inside any of us that needs to be continued. Just as there is nothing particularly transformative or helpful about any therapy that exclusively extols self-enquiry or self-help. The danger of current accounts of subjectivity are that they are intrinsically competitive and sado-masochistic. Thus, shame operates and fixes us in a place, a very painful place, where we can't access realistic hope. In order, for the shame inside us to really move, we need to look into our hearts for the love and interest we feel towards other people. For our ego ideals to travel, they have to learn to lose. In other words, we have to forget about who we are and find the Sun or rather the life-force in our desire to need, read, listen and absorb ourselves elsewhere. In the other people, or creative objects and endeavours that lead us away from the addictive celebration of our individual identity. Although our individual identity can for all of us, but especially young people, seem to be the most important thing about us. It can act to both imprison us within are shame within ourselves. And so our precious, but ultimately shameful, sense of self starts to preclude the more expansive movement of not just desire but also the hope of arriving at relationships which can broaden our horizons.

Identity, particular forms of naming subjectivity, have become an orthodoxy in our current world. Where certainty about the self trumps conversation and the freedom to express what we might think or feel. The difficulty with an ideal self and ego, these days, is the self-righteousness, that goes with it, that has become literally impossible to challenge. As the near fatal attack on Salman Rushdie in 2022 has proved, you can be easily murdered for questioning religious identity. And it takes some courage to break away from self-censorship and say anything you might think or feel about a whole range of issues in relation to trans or gender identity. When I was at university most women I knew, my friends, identified under the banner of feminism, and yet none of us agreed about anything ever. The feminism I encountered then, was energising and life affirming. I remember, as a radical midwife, some of us occupying a women's hospital near Clapham Common, which was under threat of closure. Lots of different tribes of women turned up and participated in the occupation, which I remember consisted of sitting around in groups, or 'workshops', listening to each other's stories. The miner's wives, women from Northern Ireland (fighting for peace), women from Greenham Common, black women or womanists, liberal feminists, socialist feminists, lesbian feminists all came. I even remember the rather contentious SCUM contingent, and the name horrified me – the Society for Cutting Up Men. The point was that although we didn't agree about practically anything, we were there under a common cause, to stop one of the last operational women's hospitals in London from closing. I learnt so much over those few days about the different women, and their political struggles; what constituted their communities, what and most importantly, whom these different women felt attached to.

Would such a thing be able to happen today? I doubt it. Not just because of the recent legislation banning public protest in Britain. But because even on the left, or we could say especially on the left, your tribe is now your identity and that is sacrosanct. Who you are, who you consider yourself to be, can't be questioned or explored or challenged, or met. Our political, social, ego ideals have become fixed in such an omnipotent way, and as a consequence, we are all left squinting down the keyhole. Perhaps the real shame is the collective shame that then ensues; a world, arguably, which becomes a pretty dismal place, for all of us to converse in and be.

References

Aristotle. (1985) *(n.d.)*, *Nichomachean Ethics*, translated by T. Irwin, Indianapolis, IN, Hackett.

Breuer, J. and Freud, S. (1895) *Studies on Hysteria*, in *The Standard Edition of the Complete Psychological Works of Sigmund Freud*, volume 2, translated by J. Strachey, London, Hogarth Press.

Duffy, N. (2000) *The Making of Them: The British Attitude to Children and the Boarding School System*, London, Lone Arrow Press.

Ernaux, A. (2023) *Shame*, translated by T. Leslie, London, Fitzcarraldo Editions.

Freud, S. (1905) Fragment of an Analysis of a Case of Hysteria, in *The Standard Edition of the Complete Psychological Works of Sigmund Freud*, volume 7, translated by J. Strachey, London, Hogarth Press.

Freud, S. (1914) On Narcissism, in *The Standard Edition of the Complete Psychological Works of Sigmund Freud*, volume 14, translated by J. Strachey, London, Hogarth Press.

Freud, S. (1917) *Mourning and Melancholia*, in *The Standard Edition of the Complete Psychological Works of Sigmund Freud*, volume 14, translated by J. Strachey, London, Hogarth Press.

Ishiguro, K. (2021) *Klara and the Sun*, London, Faber and Faber.

Ishiguro, K. (1989) *The Remains of the Day*, London, Faber and Faber.

Phillips, A. (2019) Shame and Attention, in *Attention Seeking*, London, Penguin Random House.

Reich, A. (1960) Pathological Forms of Self Esteem Regulation, *Psychoanalytic Study of the Child*, 15(1), pp. 215–232.

Sandler, J., Holder, A. and Meers, D. (1963) The Ego Ideal and the Ideal Self, *The Psychoanalytic Study of the Child*, 18, pp. 139–158.

Sartre, J. P. (1966) *Being and Nothingness*, translated by H. Barnes, New York, Washington Square Press.

Winnicott, D. W. (1982) *The Maturational Processes and the Facilitating Environment*, London, Hogarth Press.

3 Sadomasochism and Everyday Life

In *The Sadian Woman*, Angela Carter shows us how pornography reduces men and women to the false abstraction of sexual difference in universal, archetypal form. A simple reductive form which simultaneously removes sexuality from the social mores and conditions out of which it is constructed and denies that reality in favour of mythic universals. In this crude simplification of biological difference graffitied onto walls and toilets, of the prick and the 'fringed hole', we have the raw, and alienated symbols of our sexual difference from each other. Freud, in Carter's view, saw anatomy as our destiny, and for her that is only true in the most generalised sense. As humans we are always more complex, plural and undecided. But of course, Freud knew this, and as his life and work progressed, he became ever more aware of how ambiguous our sexuality and our many selves really are. We don't leave behind our lives when we have sex with someone, whatever the inequalities, the social and personal histories inherent in the couple; they will come unbidden into the sexual act. Pornography strips sexuality of meaning, morals, feelings, ambiguity and unknowability. Its prime function is to make this kind of deprived sexuality attractive and inviting. For Carter, the Marquis de Sade's pornographic texts are 'moral' in the sense they don't dress up pornography as romantic fiction, or private desire, they show our sexual relations as the obscene, unequal power-determined structures they are. Whereas most pornography obfuscates its function in service to the status quo, Sade is a 'moral pornographer' in Carter's view because he makes explicit the connection between obscene sex and obscene power relations. Fucking in the bedroom is completely determined by being fucked by the state, and the law, and it's a symbolically masculine privilege. In this, women are reduced to a negative function. In her analysis of Sade's literature, particularly his stories of the sisters Justine and Juliette, Carter takes these women as the Madonna/Whore stereotype by which women are viewed in society and deconstructs them. For her, Sade's Juliette, the female libertine, becomes a

DOI: 10.4324/9781003515777-3

'new woman' ruthlessly seeking power and pleasure on male terms. She attacks 'society with its own weapons'.

Carter is not excusing Sade's pornography; she sees clearly the libertine's perversion is a denial of love. If anything, she feels sorry for him, whilst applauding his failed thesis of freeing sexuality from its corruption by the powers and laws of culture. And yet, for her, pornography is the inevitable outcome of patriarchy and capitalism. Sade is both the symptom and the satirist of his generation. Irony of course being the last and arguably the most passive form of defence.

If Carter in her turn uses Sade satirically for her own feminist reconstruction of myth, Michel Foucault, following a whole line of philosophers and literary thinkers, initially wants to rehabilitate Sade as a someone who frees us from Enlightenment reason and the dialectics of power, by returning us to some kind of noble or sovereign savage:

> Through Sade and Goya, the Western world received the possibility of transcending its reason in violence, and of recovering tragic experience beyond the promises of dialectic.
>
> (Foucault, 1985, p. 285)

Foucault goes onto retract this idea in later work, but the importance of Sade for a whole history of thinkers and philosophers cannot be denied. One has to ask why? Reading Sade is, as many people have said, virtually impossible. He is unreadable, but not because of any radical insights. His work is a repetitive and boring monologue, with little imagination and his gestures to the links between the sadomasochism of the individual and the state, are not news, especially to women. I doubt they have ever been, so we have to ask not, 'Must We Burn Sade', De Beauvoir's question. But why bother to read him at all? One of the telling signs you are in the presence of perversion is how boring it is, and how compulsive it becomes for the people who are seduced by it. For Masud Khan, we have to acknowledge

> that Sade's *ecriture* is boring, oppressively repetitive and without invention – the same somatic events are concocted in a claustrophobic space with an obsessive and indefatigable insistence ... The real issue is not that pornography is immoral but that it is pathetically bad literature ...
>
> (Khan, 1989, p. 221)

Pornography, as Carter and Khan both point out, is sex in the head. And it has a specific function in persuading the reader through the text, to mentally imagine specific scenarios which supposedly stimulate sexual desire. So, pornography has nothing to do with shared experience, or we could say even self-experience. And it is quite the opposite of free association, or imaginative dreaming, being more like following a very basic literal instruction manual. As such pornography is not aimed at the instinct or our emotions but at our egos. Thus, it remains self-referential, certain and curiously depersonalised. Sade remains relevant to so many philosophers and thinkers because of his intellectual argument that sex is repressed, oppressed and regulated through power and the law. The authorities which criminalise sex, are what Sade takes aim at, and issue with. As such he has been honoured as an aesthetic thinker that combats Enlightenment reason, revealing its murderous underside.

And yet, as Lacan's ethical essay 'Kant with Sade' suggests, Sade's inalienable rights as a man, 'his right to jouissance' beyond the law, is not just the inverse of Kant's reason – his categorical imperative. Sade's 'horrible freedom' is actually indistinguishable from that law of reason (Lacan, 1989). The popularity of Sade, in other words, lies in his writing's appeal to our liberty, our universal 'rights' to our sexuality, not to be judged, or criminalised. After all, Sade's pornography is just fantasy, right? And whilst it's right that we don't burn Sade, we can see from the fatwa issued on publication of Salman Rushdie's *Satanic Verses*, and the near-fatal attack on his life in 2022, that banning books is undisputedly a barbarous act. Nevertheless, what hope really remains in Sade's prose? Are his grotesque fantasies really on the side of women's freedom? And, following on from this, is pornography and BDSM sex really sadomasochistic in a destructive form, or alternatively is it a liberation of our pleasure? Plenty of feminists and now queer theorists have tried to reclaim BDSM sex as simply the queer alternative to heterosexuality. Here, dominance and submission are a form of play, and power exchange, sometimes with a script. With strict rules in place about consent and volition. Sometimes BDSM (or 'kink' as it's called) involves a lot of pain, sometimes it's just playful.

For the advocates, BDSM creates erotic intensity, calms stress, enables closer relationships and it is seen as very imaginative. A recent book, simply titled *Kink*, is advertised as ground-breaking literature (Kwon and Greenwell, 2023). The editors R. O. Kwon and Garth Greenwell bring together popular authors in a collection that celebrates desire and sadomasochism. Their claim is that 'Kink is a way of processing trauma, and also of processing joy, of expressing tenderness and cruelty and affection and play'. The stories in this book are marketed as opening spaces between binary identities, but when you read them, the tales are familiar tropes of domination and submission and above all the erotic nature of violent humiliation. I understand that sadomasochism in sex can be very enjoyable, but what does it mean to enjoy your own or your partner's subjugation and humiliation sexually? We live an age where to question kink or BDSM in this way is to show your own unenlightened perspective. You are square, conservative or simply repressed. Just as I think people should be able to read and write whatever literature they like, I think people also need to be left alone to have whatever sex they prefer. And yet I want to question kink literature as ground-breaking. Like a lot of accounts of sex, it's both too literal and too stereotypical with fantasy, which means – it's really boring to read. Other people's sexual fantasies are surprisingly similar, and repetitive. Like dreams, it's what you feel that brings sex alive, not the script. Maybe that's just a matter of taste. More importantly, sadomasochistic sex, or any sex for that matter, is not an arena that can process or transform trauma. Turning fear into excitement might turn us on sexually, it may feel good. But it's not changing or working through that trauma in any real way; it's simply rehearsing pain, albeit in more comforting ways. A pain that was once upon a time much more disturbing.

Feminism has a long history on debating this issue, on the rights and wrongs of pornography. In the seventies and eighties radical feminists Andrea Dworkin, Catherine Mackinnon and Robin Morgan, who pronounced that 'pornography is the theory and rape the practice', were met by more liberal feminists, recently identified as sex-positive feminists, who wanted the freedom of sexuality for all woman, regardless of the BDSM practices, and in many cases in the name of them (Morgan, 1980, p. 128). One pioneer of sex-positive feminism was Gayle Rubin, whose *Thinking Sex: Notes for a Radical Theory of the Politics of Sexuality* was instrumental, and still is, for the women and queer communities who see feminism's policing of sexual pleasure oppressive. But in one sense sex-positive feminism has won, hands down. Pornography for women, gay people and the LGBT community as a whole has become celebrated rather than questioned. BDSM has become arguably not just accepted and promoted but is now seen as a vehicle of liberation from oppressive, sexual stereotyping. In fact, Rubin's most radical move has been to differentiate pornography from feminism, arguing that the latter is a theory of gender oppression whereas sexual pleasure and pornography for minority groups is another matter altogether.

I feel the same today as I did over thirty years ago about this question. Confused. On the one hand, as analyst and a therapist I see lots of women in clinical practice for whom lots of positive sex just means doing what's expected of them, whether it's individual men, or just societal/communal pressure. On the other, I think the policing of women's sexual pleasure and for the LBGT community is vicious and reproduced regularly in all kinds of prejudices. Rubin promoted her own famous BDSM organisation for lesbians in San Francisco and has always argued that sexuality should be seen as so many varieties, or differences. Thus, there is no normal sexual relationship from which perversion is a deviation. One of the problems with Rubin's arguments, is that she sees sexuality as essentially benign and about erotic pleasure. Sometimes, one person's erotic pleasure is to sadistically torture and humiliate another. Sometimes sexuality has more to do with a pleasure in cruelty; a sadism inextricable from subjugating and hating a helpless victim.

Of course, Rubin's work has been aimed at separating sexuality from the hegemonic power structures that have determined gendered relations and queer ones to. Her work has tried to wrest sexuality away from the very dilemma that Lacan points to with Kant and Sade. In insisting that sexuality be separated from gender, Rubin wanted to promote a plurality of sexualities, where one wasn't privileged hierarchically as the 'norm', over so-called more 'deviant sexualities'. Is this utopian thinking? After all none of us really likes difference. Lacan's neat deconstruction of Kant and Sade forgets that his own psychoanalysis is hopelessly intertwined with heterosexual difference and phallic institutional structures. In fact, the whole of psychoanalysis and its history is implicated in a kind of sadomasochism where genital heterosexual normativity is privileged over queer sexuality. Isn't pervert just something insulting we call a sexuality we don't like, or find threatening? And psychoanalysis is at its most perverted when it comes to mothers. Psychoanalysis has always refused to grant mothers a place as subjects and as women with their own desire. If mothers are routinely blamed in object relations theory, for their not good enough role, in augmenting stable attachment and non-narcissistic relating. In Lacanian psychoanalysis, mothers are simply relegated to the 'imaginary' a place of fantasy outside of symbolic reality, which we all have to escape from.

So, the sadomasochism of psychoanalysis lives on in its theory and practice, something I will return to later. It's no wonder that queer theory has been so suspicious of accepting psychoanalysis because of its ongoing pathologising of gay and queer sexualities. If we really think about it, sadomasochism is everywhere in everyday life. It is there in the workplace between the capitalist and his employee, it is structured between men and women, and between adults and children. Sadomasochism can be found just about anywhere where there is an imbalance of power. Where one person has institutional clout, or wealth, and the other person doesn't. With the advent of late capitalism, we are all becoming more narcissistic and more unconsciously attuned to either our omnipotence or our powerlessness. And in the particular society we live in, we can see that narcissism collapsing onto the heads of the weakest in society, especially children. In our families, parents are very big, and children are very small. If women are childrearing and not working, then there is an economic dependency on the man that makes them vulnerable. With our health Doctors have knowledge and skill, and as patients we are dependent on their good nature. And yet with our current NHS the workers are persecuted by a government system which expects their role to encompass inhuman levels of stress and exhaustion. Thus, it's not very surprising if doctors and nurses and care workers aren't always nice to their patients. Perhaps, what is more astonishing is the love and care nurses still manage to provide to sick people. Help, for the poor and for people on benefits, is dwindling amidst a rise in austerity in Britain over the last fifteen years. The resulting sadism towards the increasing number of people falling into poverty; the cruelty directed at disabled people and migrants, from any number of our governing institutions is breath taking. No longer is it really a question of where or why, do we have sadomasochism; but where or why don't we have something in place that is more hopeful or humane? In Britain, sadomasochism is structured through class, gender and race. Prejudice and the power that enables it, is not just psychological, its economic. Economic exploitation along with the omnipotence and entitlement not just of individuals, but the institutions which they inhabit, allows sadomasochism to be reproduced constantly in our everyday lives. To such an extent that we don't give a second thought to it.

In Henry James's *Portrait of a Lady*, we are presented with James's heroine, Isabel, intelligent and imaginative, who is sympathetic and spirited. She is somewhat naïve, and in representing the freedom of America juxtaposed to the corruption of Europe, Isabel is also portrayed as someone who escapes the sadomasochism of gender and class entitlement. As a rich heiress, she is free to marry whoever she chooses and her choice is both terrible and tragic, because she chooses and loves perhaps the most monstrous villain of all James's fiction, namely Gilbert Osmond. *Portrait of a Lady* is a moral story of what can happen to a woman, at the end of the Victorian age, if she happens to be too independent.

Osmond is a pervert, in the purest sense he is a sadist; a malignant narcissist, corrupt to his core. He is a man fuelled by envy and greed, a hatred which becomes more enraged through his capture of Isabel; because however much of her property, and her as his property, is acquired; her goodness and innocence remain elusive to him. And so, he makes her suffer: 'Suffering with Isabel, was an active condition: it was not a chill, a stupor, it was a passion of thought, or speculation, or response to every pressure' (James, 2003, p. 474).

Seducing and marrying Isabel for her wealth and status, Osmond is envious of Isabel, and it is this envy that drives his sadism. Coercively controlling her, he sets out to possess her completely, to destroy the independence of not just her body but also her mind. As Isabel eventually realises, far too late:

> The real offence, as she ultimately perceived, was her having a mind of her own at all. Her mind was to be his – attached to his own like a small garden-plot to a deer park. He would rake the soil gently and water the flowers; he would weed the beds and gather an occasional nosegay. It would be a pretty piece of property for a proprietor already far-reaching. He didn't wish her to be stupid. On the contrary, it was because she was clever that she pleased him. He expected her intelligence to operate altogether in his favour ... He had expected his wife to feel with him and for him, to enter into his opinions, his ambitions, his preferences.
>
> (James, 2003, p. 481)

Whilst Isabel hopelessly hangs on to her ideals of freedom and liberty, Osmond turns those ideals into dead forms he wants to accumulate. Her suffering, she hopes, no one else suspects. The exception of course is Osmond:

> She flattered herself that she had kept her failing faith to herself. However, that no-one suspected it but Osmond. Oh, he knew it and there were times when she thought he enjoyed it.
>
> (James, 2003, p. 474)

The private pain of Isabel's situation like a cloud becomes darker over time. Shadows which at first Isabel thought were just in her mind, but gradually realises are due to Osmond's presence:

> it was not till their first year together, so admirably intimate at first, had closed that she had taken the alarm. Then the shadows had become to gather, it was as if Osmond deliberately, almost malignantly, had put the lights out one by one ... She knew of no wrong he had done her; he was not violent, he was not cruel,: she simply believed he hated her.
>
> (James, 2003, p. 475)

Osmond is a sadist, but he is not a sexual sadist in Sade's sense. On the contrary, his seduction of Isabel is much more, a calculation, to destroy her psychologically and emotionally. Osmond wants to break her spirit. Sexual desire in *Portrait of a Lady* is characterised by Caspar Goodwood, almost a caricature of potent masculinity with his aggressive 'face, his figure, his presence', his 'white lightning kiss'. A kiss Isabel recoils from, sending her on the run, perhaps back to Osmond at the end of the story. The enigmatic ending of the novel has been portrayed as Isabel's frigidity in the face of real desire. And yet, we could think Caspar simply reminded her in a different more bodily way of Osmond's desire to possess her, without any heed to her own wishes. Caspar really desires Isabel, but maybe his protestation, 'I'm yours for ever – for ever and ever', was simply too much of a trap, a way of saying 'you can never ever leave me' (James, 2003, p. 634). And what kind of freedom is a desire like that?

If Osmond's sadism isn't especially sexual then what does that mean about the supposed indissoluble link between sexuality and aggression? After all, plenty of vengeful narcissists don't torture their suppliers or victims in a sexual way. For me Osmond is a sadistic pervert in the true sense of the word because he enjoys being cruel and Isabel's suffering makes him want to hurt and control her more. We can see this kind of malignant narcissism or sadism operating inside and outside of literature. Within many political leaders for example. Putin is arguably a sadist, and unarguably so was Stalin and Hitler. The ultra-right-wing Tory government in power up to 2024 was extremely sadistic and cruel, but we wouldn't necessarily posit this cruelty in sexual terms, despite the rates of sexual harassment within their ranks. What if sexuality is just a vehicle to carry what we feel and modify it? Sexuality drives our feelings and passions, but it also coats and disguises them.

Freud saw sexuality as both the essence and the cover story of what makes us human. Sexuality is there in our love and desire, but it also gets smuggled into our hate. Sadism is based on hatred, rage and a desire to hurt and master someone else. Robert J. Stoller saw all scenarios of sexual perversion as an eroticisation of hate. The perverse situation of child sexual abuse, for example, is a triumphant solution, whereby the historical humiliated child within the perpetrator disappears only to reappear in his actual child victim. In clinical practice, I hear about the sadism of domestic abusers regularly from their victims, the women that come to therapy when they have had enough, want to escape, or have become actively suicidal. Rarely, but occasionally, I find sadism in mothers, who want to hurt their children and come to therapy because they want to stop their behaviour. Men who can't find relationships with women come into therapy and their misogyny and sadistic rage towards women is based on impotence and a sense that they are entitled to their sexual desire, even when they are perfectly aware they don't like women. These men live in a state of permanent frustration, where pornography, sex with a fake or fantasy woman, substitutes for the anxieties of having a relationship with a real one.

Stoller is clear, perversion is a sort of magical trick or transformation where past trauma and anxiety becomes translated into a kind of triumphant revenge. This hostility is hidden, more or less successfully, within the erotic act. Something has to be added to the original frustration and anger to convert what was hitherto painful into pleasure: 'something new must be added to release one's body for erotic response' (Stoller, 1977, p. 103).

Stoller is faithful to Freud, inasmuch as he sees perversion as an intellectual triumph where we all to some extent change the original danger and fear we felt as children into sexual excitement we feel in the present. Freud saw the difference between neurosis and perversion, in terms of how successful our rage conversions really are. For where the pervert feels only conscious pleasure, the neurotic displays old suffering in their unconscious conflicts and symptoms. Freud argues:

> No healthy person, it appears, can fail to make some addition that might be called perverse to the normal sexual aim; and the universality of this finding is in enough to show how inappropriate it is to use the word perversion as a term or reproach.
>
> (Freud, 1905, p. 160)

So, we are all perverts, it's only a matter of degree. Stoller coins the word 'pervertic', meaning everyday perversion that explains how we move from childhood sexuality (and its traumas) to adult sexual pleasure and gratification. And yet, Stoller, is not happy with the term varieties to describe perversions. In answer to Gayle Rubin's later promotion of a variety of sexualities without hierarchy, he reminds us '"Variance" simply won't do' (Stoller, 1977, p. 103). There is simply too much tension in the dynamic conflict between how early sexual urges are inhibited, disguised and reinvented. Too much difference if you like, in the amounts of early sexual urges, how traumatically they have been felt, and the degree of violence and revenge that subsequently hides itself within our adult sexual desires and symptoms. Maybe, adult sexuality becomes a question, not simply of perversion, but of the quality of the redescription. How much or how little we can imaginatively reinvent our traumatic desires into something that is both pleasurable and not harmful?

Queer psychoanalysis has reclaimed perversion in ways that are both generative and necessary. The answer and rebellion to the normative persecution of gay people was always going to come originally from someone outside the institution of psychoanalysis. I remember 30 years ago working as a voluntary psychotherapist at our local hospital. I was yet to begin my clinical training but was halfway through a literary PhD which focused on the absence of the mother as a subject within psycho-analysis and culture. The culture in the hospital was sexist but the people were nice enough. My supervisor, who had trained at the British Institute of Psychoanalysis, taught me a lot, but I felt really frustrated at the way women and gay people were treated. Racial minority groups at that time were virtually absent in my city from psychotherapeutic care. At the polyclinic we would discuss theoretical papers in relation to clin-ical work regularly and I became increasingly angry at the way gay people would be named at the beginning of a paper as if this was simply testimony to some sort of deviance. For example, 'A homosexual woman presenting with' … One day an open confrontation occurred between me and my supervisor. At that time no one who was gay could train openly at the British Institute, and as therapists for trainees had to report to the training committee, anyone who wanted to train as a psychoanalyst at the institute had to lie to just about everyone and remain in the closet.

In the supervision group, I said 'surely we need to stop naming and pathologising people's sexuality in our papers and discussion'. My supervisor smiled benignly and said, 'Jan, you are being overly political. We don't regard homosexuality as a perversion per se, but it is an arrested stage of development.' In other words, he was calling it a per-version! I remember feeling upset and angry, but also disappointed as this was a man I respected and who had taught me a great deal. I had recently been living in a lesbian housing co-op and had worked as an agency nurse to make ends meet. A lot of the work was nursing very young men, who were dying of AIDS in isolation wards, often on their own, because of the stigma attached to them. Discrimination against gay people was at the time simply the culture of psychoanalysis, so at odds with the gay community in Brighton. These days it's trans identity that has taken the place of deviance, but that's a whole new discussion. I learnt a great deal at the Hove polyclinic, a lot of valuable clinical experience, and the wherewithal to locate an alternative training from the British Institute to become a psychoanalyst.

Is sadomasochism just an inherent part of being a person? If we are all perverts, then do we all disguise and defend against early traumas, by smuggling our rage and triumph into our sexual pleasures? Are there forms of sexuality and love that are less furious and less bent on revenge? In *Civilisation and its Discontents*, Freud (1929) suggests that it is the eros and love of fellowship based on sublimation and a binding of the ego; the reality of community and the necessity of loving one's neighbour like one-self, that helps mitigate and prevent our mutual sexual aggression and destruction of each other. But of course, as Freud points out, none of us loves our neighbours, on the whole, we hate them, so how is society supposed to collectively bind in a reality ego that can inhibit our primal sexuality? We all know Freud's pessimistic answer to this dilemma – the death drive. A move beyond the ego which is attacking and inhibiting of life and love. ·

Whether there is something like the death drive, is a moot point, but the reproduction of sadomasochism in our sexual relationships, in families, between the entitled and the ones who are not, is increasing in its severity. So what hope is there for non-violent forms of relating or sexuality. What could be a more nurturing society where vulnerability is valued rather than exploited?

Although sadism and masochism have historically been seen as two signs of the same coin, in my clinical experience they are often completely separate. As a triumphant solution, sadism is about hurting others, torturing other people to free the sadist from his past humiliations. Thus, It is fuelled by rage and revenge towards others and is found more often in men, but of course women if they are rageful and envious enough can be sadists too. Masochism in my experience is different, anger for the masochist can of course be turned in towards the self. And in the misogynist society we live in this can be a way women deal with their rage, when it is not acceptable for it to be turned towards the external world. But masochism is plural in a way that sadism isn't. Some women are masochistic, for example, because they want to heal their male partner with their love. This is perverse, because it's not based on any reality. Abused women become a sort of hospital to the mind of their abuser, and they descend into a cycle of shame and worthlessness that most commonly hurts only themselves. Gilles Deleuze makes a useful distinction between sadism and masochism, in that for him, with sadism there is a situation of absolute negation, where the supe-ego becomes monstrous and kicks out, projects the ego onto the suffering victim (Deleuze, 1997). Sadism becomes a total negation of internal conflict, where thought and reason are sexualised in a terrifying eradication of more vulnerable feelings. The Marquis de Sade to a T. All emotions here, are punished in the victim, so the sadist no longer has to feel them. Masochism, for Deleuze, is also a fairly unemotional state, but it is one that resides in a bed of fantasy as an escape from reality. If sadism partakes of the paternal order, and the revenge of the superego then masochism belongs to the maternal order, a realm of imagination, suspended from the world, a relation of idealisation between the ego and the ideal.

So, masochism and sadism are like partners who should get divorced, with no evident shared relationship, certainly no intimacy. A contract is in place, where one person doles out the torture and the other takes it. The binding nature of this contract is no-one can leave. The sadist says to the masochist, 'I can do what I like to you because I know you can't leave me'. And the masochist says, 'You can do what you like to me, because I will never leave you'. If the masochist is more heavily embedded in shame, because she is always failing her internalised mother or ego ideal, then I think there is also less neediness in the masochist. Masochistic women in my experience are often extraordinarily self-sufficient, and it's this independence and self-control which is most apparent. The ability not to need anything, which often makes these women put up with extraordinary hardship and cruelty without leaving their abusive situation. And of course, for the masochist, everything is always all their fault.

Isabel is interesting because although she fits some of the above description of masochism, in other ways she simply doesn't. She wasn't full of shame before she met Osmond, and yet she had very high ideals, which are then bitterly disillusioned. She puts up with too much, she suffers, but her plight is a pathos ridden one of Victorian society. She has married a fortune hunter, where she thought she was marrying someone entirely different. But Isabel is nobody's victim. Her refusal of the men that might rescue her, like Caspar or Lord Warburton, have been seen as a prideful character flaw. And yet Isabel, prided herself on one thing – her freedom. And so, we can't attribute a sadomasochistic dynamic to Isabel very easily, as the one thing antithetical to that dynamic is a person's freedom. Isabel is brave, fearless, innocent and that very ordinary thing, a good person. As such, she is prey to the cynical opportunism of Osmond and his mistress Madame Merle. Thus, Isabel's masochism lies in her ability to suffer passionately, in a context where she is completely divided against herself. Her masochism lies in her refusal to be corrupted and her ongoing capacity to sustain emotional pain.

If Isabel is a heroine in the truest sense, we could say a true self sense, then I suggest we have to separate not just sadism from masochism. We also have to divide masochism into the clearly destructive, self-hating, humiliated victimhood, often displayed in cultural texts of pornography, from one that is generative, in that enables us to bear our feelings.

Freud, in his paper 'The Economic Problem of Masochism' (Freud, 1905), comes finally to fully acknowledge what he first saw in his earlier *Three Essays on Sexuality*. That along with pleasure comes an excitement, a too muchness that causes pain. Sexual excitement, once it reaches a certain intensity, 'beyond quantitative limits', is met, according to Freud, with 'the excitation of pain and unpleasure':

The occurrence of such a libidinal sympathetic excitation when there is tension due to pain and unpleasure would be an infant physiological mechanism which ceases to operate later on. It would attain a varying degree of development in different sexual constitutions; but in any case it would provide the physiological foundation on which the psychical structure of erotogenic masochism would after wards be erected.

(Freud, 1924, p. 163)

There are three types of masochism in Freud's estimation. Erotogenic, feminine and moral. Erotogenic masochism, the pleasure in pain, comes first and underlies the other two. Masochism became for Freud, the great paradox or contradiction which ushered in his second drive theory. What Freud came to realise, was that if pleasure as the watch man over our lives and loves is mixed with unpleasure and pain, then masochism turns the pleasure principle into a truly ambivalent force. His answer to this paradox, namely the invention of the death drive, becomes Freud's explanation for unpleasure and masochism. It is the death drive, in Freud's view, in opposition to the pleasure principle, that is expelled outwards by the libido, as a form of sadism, whilst a remaining portion 'remains inside the organism' and is 'libidinally bound there'. This bound remainder is accordingly our original erotogenic masochism.

Such primary masochism interests me in several ways. And yet, I don't think we have to have an explanation of the death drive to explain primary masochism, we can just see the pleasure principle, the full force and excitement of it as being too much. What gets expelled from the ego is what is overwhelming, what remains bound is the pleasure/pain bedrock of our sentient lives. I want to distinguish this from Jean Laplanche's view of primary masochism in relation to an intruding maternal other, as we don't need the concept of an invading, alien, maternal unconscious to explain an infant's masochism, any more than we need the concept of a death drive. Masochism in infants is arguably the suffering they put up with in relation to the overwhelming experience of internal, instinctual demands and how those demands are met by what Winnicott would call a facilitating maternal environment.

Primary erotogenic masochism, for Freud, underpins feminine and moral masochism. But it is the last of the three, moral masochism, which Freud terms as truly secondary as it has detached itself from sexuality and becomes associated with an internalised rage or punishment of the self. With its underlying unconscious guilt this form of masochistic suffering is what we find clinically as the destructive force of self-sacrificial hate, where a person will go to any lengths to sabotage their enjoyment and those of others. In Freud's view moral masochism is nothing less than the death drive returned to haunt the ego. However, as Wilfred Bion has already noted, anything that is frustrating is either elaborated or evacuated. Moral masochism, or secondary masochism is an internalised sadism, frustration that can't be made use of fruitfully, and is then driven backwards into hatred of the self.

If secondary masochism has its partner in sadism, then primary erotogenic masochism is indivisible from primary narcissism, but the other side of what Leo Bersani would call the 'narcissistic exuberance' of this early libidinal stage. Primary masochism would as Freud argues, be an early bound portion of the infant's drive, that is able to bear suffering and pain in return for the pleasure it receives from the mother. It is the real mother who is the partner to our erotogenic masochism, for she is instrumental in elaborating our frustration in ways that enable us to bear and use our pain. The mother, not the death drive, then, a subject that psychoanalysis is still divided over. Whereas French psychoanalysis in a return to Freud, dispenses with the mother, it is the object relations tradition in Britain that has followed her, albeit in less than flattering ways. Without the external mother, the death drive becomes the explanation of masochism, but in my view the death drive is insufficient. A concept of the death drive simply can't explain how masochism can become the carrier and the elaborator, rather than the denier of psychic suffering.

This beginning masochism would be fleeting but would develop as a growing ability to tolerate frustration, pain and the possibility of having to wait. Along with Winnicott's notion of play and Bion's understanding of alpha function, primary masochism would have the ability to help elaborate suffering and need, to make it bearable and relational. How could we bear anything, without this positive ability to withstand and tolerate pain? Arguably, nothing else is possible, no ability to attach, or to access the reality principle or the depressive position. No capacity to negotiate castration anxiety or Oedipal conflicts. Certainly, no space with which to experience and tolerate the raging force of the desires we feel.

In an age where suffering is everywhere, what is most noticeable is everyone's complete incapacity to abide that pain and suffering and the consequent need to evacuate it onto or ignore it in other people. Benno Rosenburg and his work is exceptional, a French analyst who has argued for the life affirming place of primary masochism in our psychic lives. For him, masochism is our first psychic link, and he argues for the role in primary masochism, the ability to bear pain with pleasure which enables the move from pleasure to the reality principle. Rosenburg writes, 'because the pleasure principle includes masochistic pleasure and because it implies the possibility of unpleasure it can transform itself into the reality principle' (Rosenburg, 2010, p. 525).

As a French analyst, Rosenburg uses Freud's explanation of masochism as an early libidinal modification of the death drive. And so there is no need for him to consider in any depth, the role of the mother in binding the masochism of her infant. And yet if we think about what Freud is actually saying about primary masochism as the underpinning of our sexual and psychic lives, then it becomes impossible to understand how anyone could accommodate their ongoing unpleasure with pleasure without the aid of another – the mother. If we can think of all the ways the mother contains and returns, in modified form, the baby's instinctual passions, then we can see how a good enough mother helps build a positive masochism for the child. Providing flexibility, necessary space-time and the ability to wait for the growing ego. Telepathy, the unconscious communication between mother and infant, is, as I have argued in *Freudian Passions* (Campbell, 2013) not just a building of prelinguistic forms through which the child can experience feelings, it is a crucial elaboration of the child's ability to suffer and bear psychic pain in a generative way.

Isabel's masochism, her ability to suffer, is matched by her sick friend Ralph Touchett's endurance of his illness. Only at their final meeting on Ralph's death bed can Isabel admit her suffering. Ralph understands her, has always understood her at a telepathic unconscious level: 'You wanted to look at life yourself … but you were not allowed; you were punished for your wish. You were ground in the very mill of the conventional' (James, 2003, p. 622). Isabel's pain and suffering has emerged slowly in the story, a growing awareness in the face of her innocent denials. But she keeps her suffering to herself, partly perhaps through shame, but also because she wants to believe the best of her husband, when he is in fact the very worst man he could possibly be. Suffering as an emotion can't easily be worked out or elaborated on our own, we need to share our pain in order to really feel it, and in a sense go through with it. As Isabel and Ralph have their final conversation, Isabel can finally admit how unhappy she has been. As they talk, they keep returning to how pain is an inevitable part of life and their love. And thus, a part of their ability to feel alive. Isabel asks: 'Why should there be pain? In such hours of this what have we to do with pain. That's not the deepest thing there's something deeper.' And Ralph replies, 'I'm very tired. You said just now that pain is not the deepest thing. No … no. But it's very deep' (James, 2003, p.622). He goes on, 'it passes after all, its passing now. But love remains. I don't know why we should suffer so much. Perhaps I will find out' (James, 2003, p. 623).

And these are the last words we hear from Ralph before he passes. Winnicott once said he wanted to be alive when he died, and perhaps Ralph's death and Isabel's life summons the inevitable suffering and masochism in a good sense that is entailed in this aliveness. Without suffering, and the ability to feel pain, where would we be? Whom would we become? What indeed would be the point of our lives?

Sadomasochism has become in our culture (in all of its destructive forms) a mechanism where we don't have to feel very much, a way we can dumb down our emotions. It is a defence, as good as any repression, where if what we feel is too much we can limit or put a stop to it. The methods might be variously enjoyable, cruel or self-hating, and they work, although not for long, which is why they must be endlessly repeated. Sadomasochism, in short, prevents us from enduring the full range not just of what we suffer, but by extension everything we feel. There is perhaps pleasure and relief in sadomasochism, but to what end? If it narrows what we feel, then it also narrows our minds and limits what we are capable of. Isabel Archer's ability to finally share and feel her pain is the accomplishment of James's novel, and where she goes, when she flees Goodwood's embrace at the end, is not really the point. Arguably that's why the novel's ending leaves it so open as to what she does next. We might think Isabel's return to Osmond is unthinkable, or at the very least masochism at its most secondary and sadistic. But we don't know if she returns for him, or to save his daughter Pansy, or to finally leave him on her own terms. What we are told about is her final conversation with Ralph where she is finally able to experience her suffering together with someone who can really listen. Most women I see clinically in domestic abusive situations are totally shut down, being tortured on a daily basis by their abuser. And it is only when they can really express and experience their unhappiness and pain, that they are able to garner the agency to leave. So that's my fantasy for Isabel, that she does indeed leave Osmond, but of course it's also perfectly possible she doesn't, hence it's right the novel leaves it as an open question.

Because sadomasochism is created and repeated with ever increasing severity in our capitalist society. We can't just leave it to psychoanalysis to explain it. If you shame someone repeatedly don't be surprised if they respond in masochistic fashion. Sadism in people is much more linked to an inability to be vulnerable. It goes without saying that those with power and entitlement will find it easier to be sadistic and those in society who are weaker more vulnerable will be more likely to masochistically accept their lot. Because in part they have been made to feel ashamed of themselves.

As I'm writing this the illegal migration bill has just been passed in Parliament. A bill that will legislate for the persecution and state murder of thousands of legitimate refugees. Are you feeling ashamed or justified about this nightmare of our current times? Am I? It's a situation perpetuated by a cruel ultra-right-wing government, but why do so many of us find it is so frightening, given its not actually happening to us, and thus easy to disavow? And if we don't find the situation distressing what does that mean? How does it really make us feel, to witness so many vulnerable children and adults in that much distress? Disavowal relies on remaining ignorant of our fellowship and sympathy with others. Inhumanity, depersonalisation of ourselves or others is so much more difficult to do if we can really be in touch with how we feel. Sadomasochism binds people together in the most unfree way. It's comforting, more like being bound up or swaddled as a baby. But it's arguably bad for us, in that it is a mechanism which excludes everything else and enables people to shut down from their most troubling feelings, their helplessness, their shame and their guilt. Perfectly nice people will find ways of making the most awful things acceptable; like the savage attacks currently carried out against the poor, the sick or the dispossessed, in the name of austerity, the migrant bill or our cost-of-living crisis.

There is us, tightly bound together in all of our sadomasochistic practices, which are after all part of everyday life. If we put our children in a private school, or take out private medical insurance, or turn our backs on nurses campaigning for more pay, or the disabled getting more benefits, then we are buying into a system which is always whatever else it is, sadomasochistic by nature. But what does it also mean not to be a collaborator? Aren't we then in danger of becoming the kind of sacrificial masochist, the moral, self-depriver that just places the sadomasochistic relation within the self? Where do you draw the line between your entitlement and your humanity? Why wouldn't you try and protect yourself and your family before all else?

I don't know the answer to any of these questions but just ignoring them seems to be complicit, which of course we all are to varying degrees. Freud never made sadism primary, but as I've been exploring in this essay, if masochism is where we begin, it isn't just plural, it's also a force for good and for bad.

Is sadomasochism always sexual or is something that becomes sexualised as a way of making something really disturbing and traumatic more comforting? Surely there must be a degree of positive masochism in any desiring relationship, in order to bear the intensity, the range of feelings and its disturbance. And if this fundamental masochism is essential in us being able to bear our desires, to elaborate them and feel them, without pushing or projecting them outside of us. Then how do we distinguish this life force of masochism from its other more deadly counterpart? Sadomasochism, at its worst, strips sexuality of its essential need and helplessness, its humanity, and turns what should be a powerless dependency on others for our pleasure, into a self-aggrandising intellectual mastery over the flesh. And it leaves us alone. Instead of our desires being unmoored, but open to the chances and newness of life; they remain encased; locked down and isolated from what the world and the people within it can offer.

At the end of *The Sadian Woman*, Angela Carter says that it is only the possibility of love that can counter misogyny and the sacramental terror of the lonely sadist and his orgasm. For the libertine in his 'diabolical solitude', it is only the prospect of that love that can bring him to the awareness of perfect immaculate terror. It is in this holy terror of love that we find, in both men and women themselves, the source of all opposition to the emancipation of women (Carter, 1979, p. 176). But love on its own just won't do; love, and indeed pleasure, isn't something we can begin to experience without a reciprocal bearing of the inevitable suffering that goes with it.

References

Carter, A. (1979), *The Sadeian Woman*, London, Virago Press.
Campbell, J. (2013) *Freudian Passions: Psychoanalysis, Form and Literature*, Abingdon, Routledge.
Deleuze, G. (1997) *Masochism: Coldness and Cruelty*, New York, Zone Books.
Foucault, M. (1985) *Madness and Civilisation: A History of Insanity in the Age of Reason*, translated by R. Howard, London, Tavistock Publications.
Freud, S. (1905) Three Essays on the Theory of Sexuality, in *The Standard Edition of the Complete Psychological Works of Sigmund Freud*, volume 7, translated by J. Strachey, London, Hogarth Press.
Freud, S. (1924) The Economic Problem of Masochism, in *The Standard Edition of the Complete Psychological Works of Sigmund Freud*, volume 19, translated by J. Strachey, London, Hogarth Press.
Freud, S. (1929) Civilisation and its Discontents, in *The Standard Edition of the Complete Psychological Works of Sigmund Freud*, volume 21, translated by J. Strachey, London, Hogarth Press.
James, H (2003) *The Portrait of a Lady*, London, Penguin Books.
Khan, M. (1989) From Masochism to Psychic Pain, in *Alienation in Perversions*, London, Karnac Books.
Kwon, R. O. and Greenwell, G. (2023) *Kink*, London, Scribner.
Lacan, J. (1989) Kant With Sade, *October*, 51, pp. 55–75.
Morgan, R (1980) Theory and Practice: Pornography and Rape, in *Take Back The Night: Women on Pornography*, edited L. Lederer, New York, William Morrow and Co.
Rosenburg, R. (2010) (Erotogenic) Masochism and the Pleasure Principle, in *Reading French Psychoanalysis*, edited by D. Birksted-Breen, S. Flanders and

A. Gibeault, with selected material translated by D. Alcorn, S. Leighton and A. Weller, pp. 516–527, London, Routledge.

Rubin, G. (1984) Thinking Sex: Notes for a Radical Theory of the Politics of Sexuality, in *Pleasure and Danger: Exploring Female Sexuality*, edited by C. Vance, pp. 267–319, London, Routledge.

Stoller, R. (1977) *Perversion: The Erotic Form of Hatred*, London, Quartet Books.

4   The Mother of Hope

Part One

Hope has historically been framed by either religion or philosophy, and joining them is the symbolic figure of the father. Indeed, the argument for Lacan's return to Freud in psychanalysis makes this father continuous and connects psychoanalysis in particular ways with religion and philosophy. And yet if this is how the symbolic discourse of hope has been formulated, we could think that realistic hope, something that is more grounded and less intertwined with transcendental ideals of religion, knowledge and patriarchy, has been rather ignored. Hope has arguably something very real to do with mothers. The Bible tells us that the 'Mother of Hope', Mary, trusts in God's promise and so in his resurrection. Mary gave birth to the 'Light of the World', through Jesus, and so hope, our humanity, flows from her womb, or so says Christianity. And yet, we don't have to watch the film of *The Godfather* to know that hope, and our humanity, are ambivalent. We are capable of the most extreme destruction and hate. The mother of hope has become in our culture an impossible symbolic ideal of maternal love, with which woman are arguably crucified continually for not attaining. Mothering, for women, in reality is often a torn and two-sided experience, in that being a mother always divides you between your child and everything else. And yet that conflict is nothing compared to the ambivalence, idealism and hate that is directed at mothers, as people, as memories, as ideals, and at women as the Representatives. Indeed, how much we hate mothers and need them; hate them because of the extent of that helplessness and need, is always, perhaps has always been, underestimated. As children when we are frightened, when we are sick, when we are lonely, when we feel at our most mad or despondent, the person we want is our mother. However good or lovable she might be, she will always fail us. Realistic hope perhaps lies in the degrees. And so, it is not

DOI: 10.4324/9781003515777-4

very surprising that all women fail to live up to this supreme Shangri-La of perfection. But if the mother of hope, is also ours, then what does this mean in terms of hope for us, other than that it is a much more complicated and many-sided issue than theology would have us believe.

Thomas Aquinas believed that hope was both a sensible passion and a more virtuous struggle towards an 'arduous good' in relation to God. For Aquinas hope is a sensible and practical passion we share with other animals. He suggests that birds making a nest for their young have some sense that an end is possible for them. Hope is an arc into our future, but it can be purely sensory; a young child has an appetite and an expectation for what her mother can give her: an affectual hunger. This emotion of hope that connects with our senses has no particular morality attached to it. We can hope that the sun will shine tomorrow, or that we haven't missed the deadline for our tax return. Simple hope as an act is where, 'one hopes only for oneself'. And yet, if 'extraneous circumstances' intervene, we can become interested in another's hope. For example, Aquinas distinguishes between love and hope. Love, 'being a union of lover and beloved, whereas ... hope is set on personal wellbeing not that of another' (Aquinas, 1966, p. 13).

Aquinas opens up interesting distinctions between hope, desire and love. If hope as a sensible passion is selfish, then hope as a theological virtue for Aquinas is something different; it's still a movement towards what is good for us in the future, but this is a good that is difficult to obtain but not unimaginable. Presumably it hinges on the grace of God. Aquinas is clearly making a distinction between sensible hope and theological hope, but he links them. These days for many secular people, God is not so much a rational thought as a belief system. Hope in our current society moves between on the one hand sensible passions and capitalist culture, and on the other a mostly spiritual language of a hope in something that is transcendental and beyond fleshly concerns. God, like the Virgin Mother Mary, is an ideal, important for many different peoples and cultures, but he isn't knowable. The point is that he is a transcendent ideal who we can aim towards, but we can't become him or have a mutual relationship as such. Freud saw hope as religious wish fulfilment. In *The Future of an Illusion*, he likens religious belief to a child's needs and hopes for a protective and powerful father (Freud, 1927). I grew up in a religious household in the sense that my mother was a devout Christian and socialist. And for her the two were completely interchangeable. She died very suddenly when I was a 20-year-old woman, training as a student nurse. I was working in the same hospital, when she was admitted in a deeply unconscious state. She died half an hour later of a massive brain aneurysm; the shock and grief were terrible. I still remember it as one of the worst things I have ever had to cope with. My religious belief disappeared for me in the early days after she had gone. My loss of faith in God was, or so it seemed to me, immediate. I had been angry with my mum in a normal adolescent way, and rather rebellious with what I saw at the time as her sacrificial 'good' works for the community, and worldwide development, namely Oxfam and Christian Aid. And yet despite this, in the early days of my grief which felt ubiquitous, I grasped one thing very clearly. The good thing I believed in, wasn't located in God, for he no longer existed, but that good thing had existed within my mum. However, furious I had been at times with her. My unconversion had consequences within my family. I remember my Uncle Alan on my father's side, saying one day:

> It's all very well giving up on God, but one day you might not be able to afford that non-belief. Think of soldiers in the war, with all the bombs flying over. Don't you realise how grateful they would have been for their belief. How indispensable it would have been for their hope and survival?

I don't remember what I said in return, but it made no difference to how I felt. I didn't miss God; there was no hope left in him; it was my mother who had gone missing.

D. W. Winnicott, in a clinical vignette of a patient, describes how the work entailed a search for an original scream that became the 'non-event of every session'. A scream that could not be experienced because of the moments in childhood where the infant's cries were unmet. The scream, Winnicott suggests, the patient was looking for 'is that last scream just before hope was abandoned'. He continues, 'Since then screaming has become no use because it fails in its purpose' (Winnicott 2016a, pp. 96–97).

Hope, for Winnicott has something to do with mothers which is not idealised or transcendental. For Winnicott, the loss of hope is also a loss of freedom to creatively think and live. He writes: 'the essence of cruelty is to destroy in an individual that degree of hope that makes sense of the creative process' (Winnicott, 1990, p. 233). Winnicott's sense of hope links to the idea that we are born into the world with extreme needs that we cannot meet on our own, and how those needs are met by our particular mothers, is crucial to our ongoing wellbeing, and creative living.

The importance of mothers leads to their idealisation and denigration; they are either divine or abject. Nowhere rehearses this splitting more than within the history of psychoanalysis. Within French psychoanalysis the mother is either a toxic unconscious influence, or a mad imaginary dream that we have to escape from. And within the British school she is idealised as a function without any consideration of what her personal subjectivity and history brings to the table. Two female analysts and philosophers, both French, have tried to resurrect more creative thinking about mothers in psychoanalysis. Julia Kristeva's 'Stabat Mater' (Kristeva, 1986a) is a rehearsal and history of the cult of the Virgin Mary, interspersed with a poem about her own maternal experience. In an age where Christianity and the cult of the Virgin Mary are dwindling, Kristeva asks what will replace Mary as a sublimation and symbol for maternity? In this discourse the mother, and Mary, occupy a privileged and sacrificial place in relation to the socio symbolic. In her accompanying essay, 'Women's Time', Kristeva (1986b) suggests the danger of certain feminisms, is in thinking they can challenge this paternal symbolic and remain outside of it, thus threatening themselves with paranoia and psychosis.

Faithful to Lacan's theory of a paternal symbolic, where language and separation from the mother is always signified by a male term, Kristeva puts sacrifice for the woman, and for all of us more generally, as the only way towards a hopeful, ethical and sane existence. But we could ask why sacrifice for anyone is the route towards hope and ethics. Luce Irigaray's understanding of the place of the mother is very different, and in her direct challenge to the phallocentric constructs of Lacanian theory, she posits a much more fluid relationship between mother and daughters; a sort of ongoing dance of being together and then apart. Irigaray's exploration of how daughters separate from mothers is extremely interesting. She takes issue with Freud's famous fort/da game, as the story that psychoanalysis tells itself about separating from the mother. Freud observed in his little grandson, Ernst, a game whereby the child masters the absences of his mother through chucking a cotton reel attached to string out of his cot and saying 'o-o-o' (which Freud took to be 'Fort!', meaning 'Gone!'), and then pulling it back with pleasure crying 'Da' (meaning 'Here!'). Freud refers to this as the fort/da game, where the reel is far away and then near, arguing that this mastery of the mother's absence is also the means with which the child enters language and meaning. In Lacanian parlance it is nothing less than entry into the symbolic order (Irigaray, 1987, p. 97).

Irigaray suggests that girls don't separate from their mothers in such an extreme and linear way:

> She does not play with the string and the reel that symbolise her mother, because her mother is of the same sex as she is and cannot have the object status of a reel. The mother is of the same subjective identity as she is.
>
> (Irigaray, 1987, p. 97)

The little girl can't objectify the mother in the way a boy can because she is the same sex as her mother. Irigaray imagines the girl's distress at the mother's absence, losing her power, even the will to live and becoming anorexic. However, a positive response for the girl happens when she finds the game of the doll. Playing with the doll organises a symbolic space for the girl, allowing her to create a territory of her own in relation to her mother, for the doll is not 'an object in the way that a reel, a toy car, a gun etc are'. But my response to this is why can't the doll game be for boys too? Surely a separation that master's the mother and reduces her to an inanimate object isn't good for any child. We could, arguably, draw a straight line between the fort/da game and the pastime of pornography. Games with dolls are imaginative, you can play at being the mother, looking after the doll, even being cruel to the doll; you can also be the doll. Indeed, there is an identification with the mother in playing with dolls which doesn't just help girls create their own space-time, it is also an imagining of the mother's personal subjectivity. Why can't this possible imaginative reverie be for boys? So much of my clinical practice with certain men is about the huge misogyny and resentment they feel against women, which goes back to what they feel they have been deprived of by their mothers. Maybe hope for men, when it comes to hating women, is to encourage boys to imagine, to elaborate on their many identifications with their mothers? Not just what they needed and lost, but what her personal history entailed. Maybe the generative identification with the mother and her body in childhood, that boys are schooled to leave so abruptly, could be elaborated on in ways that made their separation less stark and violent. But of course, for this to work, fathers and adult men must encourage this sympathetic identification with the mother and be a masculine role model accordingly. Having the mother as the only locus of powerful identification could encourage a sort of envious mimicry, where nothing is really internalised, and the copying remains misogynistic and mocking. We only have to think of Norman Bates in *Psycho* for this depressing rendition.

The film *Barbie* (2023) is a feminist and humorous take on the doll, which moves between critique and advert for the Barbie, asking the question, 'Are the dolls oppressive or empowering?' I remember my daughter when she was very young at the heart of my feminism in the eighties and early nineties. I dressed her in blue dungarees, and we went to Greenham Common and on political marches. When she was about three, rebellion ensued. She asked to wear dresses, told me her favourite colour was pink and demanded – yes, of course – a Barbie! The only thing I took issue with in the film was the beginning, which showed a lot of toddler girls playing with baby dolls at the seaside, and all they can do is play mothers. Then a huge Barbie appears, and they smash all their baby dolls against the rocks, breaking the dolls' limbs and breaking off their heads, as they look up in awe and worship of the older Barbie they want to become.

Of course, some of this is just kids growing up and throwing away childish things. And yet the feminist message in the film was clear: playing at mothers is babyish, and boring, whereas Barbie by comparison is an empowered sexually exciting woman, who all little girls want to become. Such a dividing line between feminism and motherhood seems, today, still as indelible as ever.

For all her imaginative thinking in relation to the mother–daughter relationship, Irigaray, like Kristeva, ends up with an ethics situated in the transcendental. Although for her it's a female divine, rather than a paternal symbolic that mediates and symbolises female desire. And it seems that most ethical debates, both within philosophy and outside of it, agree with situating ethics and hope within a transcendental religious relationship, which marks difference. Take the two philosophers Simone Weil and Emmanuel Levinas, on the face of it very different thinkers, dedicated to thinking through questions of ethics and equality between individuals. Levinas situates hopefulness in God, as the infinite relationship we have with the 'Other', both a response and a responsibility which is simultaneously a 'face to face' with each other on a sentient level (Levinas, 1992, pp. 82–84). For him, our experience of another is an absolute responsibility for him or her in their alterity and difference. Simone Weil's philosophy departs from early Marxism and anarchism to find hope in Christianity and the freedom and truth that only this impersonal and individual relationship to God can accomplish. For her, all truth and goodness become located in our impersonal relation to God, and we have to allow this religious love to eradicate the selfish 'I' of our egoism: 'Everything without exception which is of value in me comes from somewhere other than myself' (Weil, 2005, p. 103).

Weil places sacrifice and self-abnegation at the centre of our ethical being. Self-discipline remains at the heart of her thinking in a manner that is extreme and to my mind depressing. If we go back to the distinction made by Aquinas between the experience of hope and its disposition as a religious virtue as a difficult stretching towards what is good, we can see there is quite a gulf between what we might feel as hope, and the hope we should be striving for – namely a moral good. Aquinas doesn't attempt to bridge this gap as he describes youths and drunks as 'the kind of fools that lack deliberation'. So, hope for Aquinas is delusional without God to stretch for and yet for Freud it is precisely this reaching towards a religious father which is delusional and childish (Aquinas, 1966, p. 13).

Is all hope madness? And why do we need a transcendental relationship with a theological father figure to make hope something good or even realistic? A concept of the female divine, is no real advancement on a Christian God, or a paternal symbolic, for that matter. We only have to look at the media coverage of Russell Brand's unsurprising misogyny, to watch him claim his worship of female divine power, as a ruse to seduce the teenagers he solicited. The religious understanding of hope goes back further historically to the theological virtues of faith, hope and charity. Whereas more contemporary ways of positioning hope are to link it as simply another word for desire. And yet realistic hope, in my view, hope that is not delusional or magical must be something more ordinary and less extreme or fundamental. What I mean by this is that when we believe in God there are no maybe's; or with desire we don't just want something in moderation. Belief, like desire exists, or it doesn't. The problem with putting our hope in a religious deity or just in a transcendental relationship means putting our faith in the extraordinary, in a being that is superior in power, or virtue. Whatever we think God is, and however much we set store by his or her goodness, one of the common things that is said about religion is that it helps us be good because it enables us to make sacrifices. Although religion arguably offers complex positive things to people, cultural belonging, community, generosity to others etc. the idea that sacrifice helps us love others is surely false; for sacrifice doesn't make us better as people, it just makes us cross and full of hate. It is for example always very bad for mothers and therefore children. Sacrifice won't help us alleviate climate change, which is arguably why the UK's former prime minister, Rishi Sunak, promised us we could reach 'net zero' without having to give anything up, like diesel cars, gas boilers or even gas oil fields. But giving up doesn't have to be sacrificial. Adam Phillips has asked, 'Why not give it up?', suggesting that giving up might be just another way of reconsidering past desires, or other possible options that have been precluded (Phillips, 2024, p. 27). If climate change is going to destroy everything we know and love, and that's a truth. Then, why wouldn't we want to consider losing our cars or tolerate the unreliability of heat pumps. It is not until we experience the pain of being left out, that we realise we are able to move. And so, loss of the things we most value, like commodities, youth and even health; if they are lost with a view to what they make way for, can help us find new ways to preserve the world, or even find contentment with ageing.

Winnicott talks about hope as a formative experience at the beginning of life, which can extend to freedom and creative living. And although he believed that hope was as fundamental as religious belief or desire. Even more so, as we can't live a creative life without it. Winnicott also saw hope as a transitional state. For hope to work, it has to move, between the child and the mother, and between fantasy and reality. In his paper 'Transitional Objects and Transitional Phenomena', Winnicott (2005) relates how the 'good-enough mother' begins with 'an almost complete adaptation to the child's needs'. As time goes on this adaptation becomes less exact and less complete, giving the infant ability over time to 'deal with her failure'. This failing adaptation of the mother is a good thing, because it allows the child to find reality and the objects pertaining to it, without becoming too devastated or traumatised. The complete adaptation of the mother at the start of a baby's life provides the infant with an 'illusion' that the breast is part of herself, and although Winnicott doesn't call it this, he is talking about hope. At the start this illusion is magical and omnipotent, the breast is a subjective phenomenon for the baby, under her (or his) magical control. And so, the next task for the mother is in disillusioning the child, but 'she has no hope of success' if the preceding illusion or hope has not been present. The mother's breast, in other words, becomes created again and again by the infant through his need and hope, as something subjective. Over time, through weaning and disillusionment, the breast can have a more real and objective existence for the child.

The disillusioning of the child is a delicate process, whereby frustrations have to be born. And we can see that the illusion Winnicott speaks of, as a form of hope, continually moves from the subjective, extraordinary creation of the object – to its disappointing companion in the real world. This moving object, for the child, is one that is created and then found differently again and again. The importance of this moveable entity is that it is never just subjective fantasy or hard-edged reality but a mixture of both. As Winnicott so famously said, we must always agree with the baby 'that we will never ask the question. Did you conceive of this or was it presented to you from without?' (Winnicott, 2005, p. 17).

Transitional objects move as they become elaborated from breasts, to blankets, to soft toys and dolls. Thus, transitional objects, and the experience that accompanies them, turns hope into a much more liminal concept than has hitherto been acknowledged. Instead of delusional fantasy, or a fundamental belief, hope becomes a paradox of what is imagined and what is real; of what we want, and what we can't have. It makes disappointment less final, but it also turns hope's range into something more limited, preventing it from becoming simply omnipotent flight or magical thinking.

Having to think of hope as something that is always on the move, appearing and then disappearing could make it sound unbearably tantalising. Like an unbearable tantalising mother. And yet, for Winnicott, this move between illusion and disillusion is precisely the outcome of our successful dependence on a mother. A dependence, if consistent enough, which helps transform what is unbearably frustrating into the freedom of our alive continuity or living. There is no hope without disappointment, but no freedom without our ability to hope. If hope starts out as the most omnipotent thing about us, for it to work in a reasonable and realistic way; our hope, along with us, has to learn to lose and shapeshift. This means, I think, not just getting used to repeated disappointment. Rather, imagining the whole dynamic of illusion and disillusion changing the nature, not just of what we can conceive of, but the nature of what we find to be actually there. In other words, hope has to move and change in relation to its differing companions.

Motherhood of course is accorded great importance in Winnicott's work, and although Winnicott references how natural it is for women to be good mothers, he doesn't really dwell on how tough it might be for them, although of course he writes plenty about how difficult it is to be a child. I've worked with mothers in different ways for most of my life, and motherhood was also the centre of much of my study when I was a literary academic. Maybe my interest stems from losing my own mother so young. But mothers are also such interesting people to listen to, especially about their children. And this is because they intuitively know their children so well and love them so much. A mother's love for her child is a wild thing. There is something untamed about it. Not because mothers are necessarily too passionate about their children, but because their love is so wide and deep.

Of course, there are so called bad mothers and as a culture we are fascinated by them. The kind of mothers who hurt their children and are deemed to enjoy it. Estela Welldon, a psychoanalyst and writer, is especially focused on women who are very ambivalent about their children, labelling them perverts. Whereas men direct their perversions onto other people, women, in Welldon's view, direct their perverse desires inward, into their bodies and onto their children. In her book *Mother, Madonna, Whore*, Welldon considers the predicament of the baby girl, more difficult than the boy, because the girl, in her view, is born to someone 'who is not her "true" sexual object' (Welldon, 1988, p. 69). In other words, mothers don't desire and love their little girls in the way they do boys. As blatantly untrue as this is. Anybody can see, if they haven't experienced it, the strong sensual connection baby girls have with their mothers; and it's a cathexis that is a two-way street. We can also notice how the heterosexual sweep of most historical psychoanalysis is present here in Welldon's words, aligning heterosexuality with successful mothering. If, as Welldon suggests, girls suffer more because their mothers are not their natural sex object, then what does this mean for lesbianism, or queer sexuality in general? We are perilously close to the old prejudices of queer sexuality being a perversion. In another publication, with a chapter entitled 'Mothers as the Creators of Sadomasochism', Welldon explores the case of Beverley Allitt in 1993, a student nurse who suffered from anorexia, with a history of self-harm, who went on to murder some of the babies under her care. For Welldon, the perversion of Allitt's 'self-mutilation' should have been enough to point to the dangers of letting her work as a nurse; a perversion that signalled back to early deprivation in mothering and forward to her role as a serial killer of the babies in her care (Welldon, 2002). Self-harm and anorexia are not signs of a perverse character, however much they might be seen as perverse acts. In fact, they are quite common symptoms for teenage girls in our society, in response to numerous psychological conflicts. The pressure girls can feel today and put on themselves for not being good enough is enormous, and the difficulty they feel in becoming women, expressing their feelings, especially their rage. Sacrifice and self-deprivation are central to both anorexia and self-harm and show the punishing ego-ideals that accompany so many teenage girls into adulthood. In Hadley Freeman's wonderful book *Good Girls: A Story and Study of Anorexia*, she describes the obsessive self-hate and the struggle teenage girls undergo in developing into women:

> I wish we were better at telling girls that there are endless ways to be a girl, and I wish we were better in convincing them that there are endless ways to be a woman. And most of all, I wish we the grown woman were better at believing it ourselves … Because how else will the younger generations stop hating themselves if they're learning it from us? I wish we could tell them that starving themselves to be perfect is as nonsensical as punching themselves on the face to turn orange. But we don't. Not enough. Not yet.
>
> (Freeman, 2023, pp. 268–269)

One of the phenomena I saw as a midwife when I was quite young, and have continued to witness throughout my career as a therapist, are the women who have had difficulty mothering, and who can't, as it were, mother through instinctual memory. Instead, these mothers imagine what hasn't been given to them and give it to their children. I have seen this with the brutally poor, drug addicted women, living on deprived housing estates of Niddrie and Craigmillar in Edinburgh. Some of these women were inadequate mothers, they were all addicted to heroin and a lot of them were sex workers. And yet some of them, and this surprised me at the time, were really good mothers to their children. They wanted their children to have something different, a life they hadn't been able to experience. I have also seen this transformative action of mothering with the more middle-class women who have come for therapy in very different circumstances. What you had from your mother does not determine how you will mother. And of course, imagining what you haven't had and then providing it for your baby is difficult. But then motherhood is not easy anyway; it involves struggle and suffering, as well as pleasure and joy. One of the things, that enables mothers to negotiate the obstacles they face, is the strength of the love they feel for their kids.

I guess, in response to Welldon, I would say, isn't it remarkable just how well so many women mother? Of course, some mothers will be damaging and cruel, but they are not the majority. What we wanted from our mothers, and more importantly, what we feel we were owed, and we didn't receive, is another matter. Hopes are always exorbitant when it comes to mothers, and so it is perhaps inevitable that they give way to grudges. In 2023 the trial of Lucy Letby came to a close, and the familiar rhetoric of female serial killers raised its head. Letby was found guilty of murdering several premature babies under her care, as well as attempting to murder several others. Dr Marissa Harrison, writing in the *Guardian*, argues that we must be able to recognise that 'sometimes the monster is a vanilla nurse who took dance lessons, fancied a staff doctor, and had teddy bears, fairy lights and a polka dot dressing gown in her bedroom' (Marrison, 2023).

Labelling this woman as evil means we lose sight of the fact that Letby, however appalling her actions, was someone clearly in need of a lot of help. I worked for periods of several months in neonatal units, at Guy's Hospital in London and at the Sussex County Hospital in Brighton. Of the work, I remember two things very clearly. First, how incredibly fragile these premature babies were. I can still picture the tiny babies, barely human beings lying in incubators under brightly coloured revolving animal mobiles. I remember the sheer weight of responsibility, where you could easily take off a piece of the baby's skin, along with micropore tape securing the feeding tube, without the exercise of extreme care. The second thing I remember were the parents, always mothers, sometimes fathers as well, losing their minds with anxiety over their children and worrying whether they would live.

Lucy Letby had been in a premature baby unit herself. It was one of the reasons she gave for wanting to work with these particular children.

My fantasy is not that Letby is an evil monster, but that she had a mother whose anxiety started in the prenatal unit and didn't stop. Growing up with that level of maternal anxiety and trauma can produce huge amounts of rage in children, because the child feels unseen for who he or she is. Maternal anxiety can be so preoccupying that other important things about a child go unnoticed. Lucy Letby's killings might have been a revenge on the anxious mothers in the unit, and a revenge against the anxiety of her own mother. But it might also have been an urge to destroy what had been suffocating about her own childhood, and the unbearable vulnerability that was attached to her mother's love. But there is also another equally disturbing view on Letby's case, and that is, she might be innocent. She has always claimed to be, and there is mounting evidence from numerous specialists that insufficient attention has been given to the lapses and underfunding of NHS care that made these babies more susceptible to sudden unexplained deaths. Some of the prosecution rested circumstantially on Letby being the only nurse present when the deaths took place, but this evidence has already been compromised by the finding that the cameras picturing the other nurses leaving the unit were actually capturing their return, and so compromising any certainty of the situation. Also, the evidence of her supposed admission to the killings was taken from Letby's counselling sessions shortly after her arrest and they do not make for a compelling case at all, demonstrating guilt over her lack of care of the babies involved, rather than guilt because she had actively wanted their deaths. As much as we find it horrifying that a young nurse might murder the babies in her care, it is equally horrific to think that we might have convicted an innocent woman, because we can't believe the NHS is really that bad, or that stereotyping a female nurse killer of babies as a monster is so easy, merely the other side of our preferred way of seeing ideal women (i.e. nurses like Letby) as saints.

If we are to believe, as Welldon wants us to, that motherhood 'provides an excellent vehicle for some women to exercise perverse and perverting impulses towards their offspring', the question is surely the word 'some'. Because, of course, 'some' women want to hurt their children and do, and some nurses, maybe Letby, maybe not, harm where they should care. It's an intolerable thought, because these are the people we entrust with our most helpless selves. For this trust or hope to be betrayed is thus seen as unforgivable. Perhaps the more interesting question is why mothers and nurses don't do more harm. Why not, given the power they hold, and therefore can wield, over their children and patients? As a society we aren't particularly nice to people we regard as too vulnerable or exposed. And yet mothers and nurses not only choose, but are frequently, and reliably, kind to the vulnerable children and adults they look after. There is a generosity at work, that we so easily take for granted and never question. And maybe we should think about this and be more curious, because it's not a hope and trust we bestow so readily on other adults, in other walks of life.

A mother's perversity, in Welldon's view, arises from feelings of power and control over those in her care. And yet the most common feelings I see in mothers (apart from their intense love and anxiety) is their ambivalence and vulnerability. Not because they don't love their children enough, but because they are divided, eternally, between meeting the needs of their children and everything else.

Part Two

In *The Lost Daughter* by Elena Ferrante, Leda is a mother of two daughters, who have flown the nest as young women, to live with their father, and her divorced husband. Feeling, not loss, but unexpectedly light and free of her two daughters' demands, Leda travels to the coast in Italy for a holiday. One the beach she becomes mesmerised by a young mother and her small daughter, playing together. Leda watches the mother and child in a bodily embrace, 'touching noses, spitting out streams of water, kissing each other'. As they laugh together and hug in the water, she notices they are both playing with a doll together with much enjoyment and pleasure. They dress and undress the doll, bathing her in the green beach pail and then drying her. Smothering her in sun lotion so she won't burn, as though she was a real child. Leda observes the mother's prettiness, but it is in her undivided desire for her daughter, in her motherhood that she becomes remarkable (Ferrante, 2021, p. 19).

The child Elena goes missing for a while on the beach and Leda manages to find her and return her to the extended family she belongs to. Nina the mother comes over to thank her, saying of her ordeal, 'I thought I would die' (Ferrante, 2021, p. 43). Elena has been found but is not happy, she is desperate and crying because she has lost her doll. Unbeknownst to Nina, and the rest of the family, Leda has impulsively stolen the doll, hiding it in her handbag. Back home, Leda reflects guiltily on her actions, remembering her own favourite doll as a child, whom she had taken great care over. As a child Leda had wanted to play with her mother's body and turn it into her doll. But as Leda recalls, her mother wasn't comfortable being the doll, she would get anxious and irritated. Although she laughed, she pulled away from Lena, getting more and more cross as the daughter put ribbons in her hair, washed her face and behind her ears, undressed and attempted to redress her (Ferrante, 2021, pp. 46–47).

When Leda, in turn, becomes a mother, she is determined to be an unresentful doll for her eldest daughter. Patiently letting Bianca drag her into the playhouse, even though Leda is exhausted, she allows her daughter to minister to her as though she is sick but obtains no joy from the game. Passive and exhausted, Leda, finds being a 'good' mother depressing and turns avidly to her literary work to ease her mind. Feeling a pang of guilt about her ambivalence, Leda gives Bianca her favourite childhood doll. But, instead of treasuring it, the little girl uses the doll as a chair, and scribbles all over it. Lena's fury when it erupts is cruel and pleasurable. She throws the doll over the balcony and they both watch through the bars, Leda triumphant and Bianca frightened, as the doll gets mauled and mutilated by the passing cars.

Ferrante's *The Lost Daughter*, although brilliant, is a disturbing book to read, because it spells out the maternal ambivalence at stake for women, and how split they feel between meeting the needs of their children and themselves. When Leda comes across the younger mother Nina and her daughter, she is envious of their creative play because their game with the doll, embodies a passion and a mutuality that has been missing, in her mind, with her own daughters, and of course with her mother. Leda's guilt and thus her 'crime', is that after years of feeling her life sacrificed to mothering, she leaves her children for three years to find her-self again.

When I was teaching at Sussex University, many years ago, I taught a course entitled 'Motherhood and Representation'. In those days if you had done a PhD and were employed to teach you could create and choose pretty much what you wanted. That was a freedom. The course was very popular and brought together young and mature students (mainly women), in a way that I hadn't anticipated. The younger students understood, and identified with, the role of the daughter, and the older women with the mother. There were arguments and alliances. The last seminar was on mothers that leave. And the consensus was unanimous, leaving your children, as a mother, is just something you don't do; no-one recovers. I still think this is true. Although the case I put forward then and still posit now is why can't they? Fathers leave all the time, and we think nothing of it. And so Leda's history, her act of leaving her children, isn't just a tragedy for her and her children. It's an indictment on what Adrienne Rich called the 'institution of motherhood'. The ideology and infrastructure of our society, of so many societies, that determines the sacrificial nature of mothering.

Nina is not immune to the frustrations of being a mother and adopts Leda, the older woman, as an ego ideal representing everything she wants to be, and yet feels prohibited from achieving, because of her marriage when she was a teenager, her lack of education and her low self-worth. As she admits her ignorance and self-contempt to Leda, she announces, 'The only true thing I want is to escape' (Ferrante, 2021, p. 138).

Nevertheless, Nina's suffering does not seem to diminish or dent her love for her child. Her need for escape manifests at the end of the novel, as a desire to come and stay with Leda, in Florence. 'Will you help me', says Nina, and Leda's rejection is to cruelly reveal herself as the doll thief (Ferrante, 2021, p. 138). Nina's hope in Leda is shattered: 'Why?' she asks simply. 'I don't know', says Leda. Nina is filled with incredulous rage; how can Leda read and write all day and not know. How could she have possession of the missed and missing doll, and hold onto it, knowing how much Nina was at a loss at how to act and how to comfort and repair the immense loss, that the missing doll meant to her child. Elena was driving her mother mad because she expected her mother to magically restore the doll, whilst Leda, remained quiet in the full knowledge she was in possession of the doll, yet refused to speak, or act. Even though the distress of both Nina and Elena were ongoing and obvious, Leda sadistically withheld (Ferrante, 2021, p. 139). Leda finally responds to Nina's howl of outrage with 'I'm an unnatural mother', and we see the fury and pain, which Leda doesn't really comprehend in herself, boil over in the younger woman. Nina's parting shot is to stab and wound Leda, in the side, with a hat pin.

On the second page of this short novel, Leda reflects to herself and to us, that the most difficult matters to talk about are the ones we least understand about ourselves. Leda is only half aware of her anger that has episodically arisen in the past, as 'small alarming' moments when caring for her children. As readers we are made aware of the sadistic rage that breaks out, against her daughters particularly Bianca, who refuses to be the victim to her mother's rages. One memory of really hurting her daughter returns to Leda. She is at home trying to write, with the children trying to distract her, at her feet. Bored Bianca, wanting her mother's attention, comes and slaps Leda on the ear. Leda, her thoughts, and what at the time feels like her entire ambition and career, interrupted, hits her daughter back. Leda's narration is an expatiation of the memory in merciless detail. She remembers her child's tears under her fingertips as she repeatedly hits her. Although the blows are gentle, they are controlled and deliberate. There is no possibility that this act of reproval is educational, it becomes a real demonstration of controlled violence (Ferrante, 2021, p. 73).

Leda steals the doll from Nina's child, because she has suffered a deprivation in leaving and abandoning her children, one that no doubt leads back to her own experiences when she was young. Winnicott, in his paper 'Delinquency as a Sign of Hope', describes how the act of stealing in adolescent boys, is actually a sign of hope. Stealing, for the adolescent is a quest for restitution. An act of aggression whereby the child hopes to be able to take someone who will listen back to the moment of deprivation or to the phase in which deprivation became consolidated into an inescapable reality. The hope is that the boy or girl will be able to re-experience in relation to the person who is acting as psychotherapist the intense suffering that followed immediately the reaction to deprivation.

(Winnicott, 2016b, p. 95)

The problem for Leda, is that the earliest deprivation has become overlayed by the privations she has visited on her own children. One of the things that Winnicott stresses is that the delinquent wants to get back to a time before the trauma. A time when she or he could use objects creatively. And so, Leda's envy of Nina and Elena's game with the doll, her greed if you like, for what has gone missing, opens the way for the hopeful and sadistic act of stealing the doll. Would Leda have hit her children, or left them, without the sacrificial institution of mothering within which she lived? It's unknowable, but one of the things I've noticed in my work with mothers is that the more sacrifice is around, the more rage is produced.

When women come into therapy because they want to hurt their children and are frightened by their feelings, they often describe honestly the feelings of pleasurable triumph, the sadistic rage it gives them, but they also talk about it coming from outside of them as a sort of dispossessed force. The work is to get them to own their rage and their original feelings of abandonment often with their rageful mother when they were little. The rage is a triumphant re-enactment, the pain behind it takes longer to work through. And of course, it is a massive act of hope that any of these mothers show up for therapy at all, with all the shame involved.

In this chapter, I have been considering what a reasonable case of hope would look like. What does this really mean? Hope in God, for many people, is a faith that sustains them and makes their lives more meaningful and loving or simply better. For others religious hope makes them fanatics, like the attempted murderer of Salman Rushdie. So maybe it's not simply what we hope for, but how we hope. It's an important question: what does hope give us, personally or politically? Our most fervent wishes might make us feel good, and they might help us bear to go on living. And yet hope is paradoxical. In the Greek myth of Pandora's Box, Pandora is given a jar or box by Zeus and instructed not to open it. Being unable to control her curiosity Pandora opens the jar, and the seven evils of the world fly out. Pandora slams the jar shut and the last evil, hope is trapped inside. Is the hope evil because of its propensity to be false? Or is the hope left in the jar, like Pandora, both a blessing and a curse? For Winnicott, hope begins and ends, quite simply with our mothers. It exists in the potential space between the child and the mother, what he calls the transitional space, where creativity and freedom of living are experienced. Another word he uses for this is playing. Playing is the movement between inner and outer reality, it is the space where all creative objects are imagined and found.

For Leda, when she sees Nina and Elena playing with the doll on the beach, her envy is a form of recognition for what she has lost. The sacrifice of the ideology and infrastructure of mothering – its institution, has veiled and prevented her for being able to connect with the passionate experience that motherhood can be, rather than a sort of superego obligation or injunction. Leda's act of stealing the doll, in my fantasy, is an attempt to get back to a time on the beach, when she was younger, before the trauma and subsequent loss of hope. A place where playing with dolls and creating yourself as a companion, rather than the master of your mother, goes together with the mother's ability to play back. Maybe that's what I find disturbing about the young children smashing up their baby dolls on the beach in the film Barbie. It's because they make way for a Barbie, in all her commodified glory, who has never needed anything, certainly not a mother or indeed a child. And where's the creative play in that?

How easy it can be for some mothers to play with their children, and I don't just mean specific children's games. The play Winnicott is talking about is an ability to be with your child, in a communication that acknowledges them. It's something you can do on the sofa watching crap television together, but it's also about paying attention to what they feel and think. Sacrifice for mothers gets rid of play. Just as mastery in the cotton reel game gets rid of the mother. It is not unrelated to consider how Winnicott disposes of the obstacle in the fort/da game (the reel) and settles for the open-ended play that can be initiated through the string. His exploration of children's feelings through the famous squiggle game. And so, we have to ask what would psychoanalysis have been like, if Freud had been a woman, or indeed a mother? What would have happened to all our sacrificial separation stories for the child? And what would it have meant not to have objectified the mother as an insentient thing and sent her into oblivion? What if psychoanalysis had had the game of the doll instead as its originating game or play? A play that instead of simply chucking the mother away and bringing her back under a kind of omnipotent control, could imagine and enact all sorts of imaginary games with her. Being her, nursing her, sometimes scribbling on her. And as I've said before, I don't think this is just a game for little girls. Arguably it's a play we all potentially learn because it is where we start.

For Winnicott, creativity belongs to that early space of play. The transitional space where the mother, and all objects that follow her, are made up and found differently over and over again. Mothers love their children as part of themselves, which is why they can give up and give away so much to them without it feeling sacrificial. For however much we expect unreasonable amounts of sacrifice from the mother, it's also fascinating how much devotion a mother can extend to her child without experiencing that care as sacrificial. Freud explained this as just another version of our childish narcissism. Parents, Freud suggests, want the lives for their children they didn't have:

> The child shall have a better time than the parents; he shall not be subject to the necessities which they have recognised as paramount in life. Illness, death, renunciation of enjoyment, restrictions on his will, shall not touch him.
>
> (Freud, 1914, p. 91)

For 'His Majesty the Baby', and the parental love that creates it, is nothing more, in Freud's view, than the parent's narcissism born again, which, transformed into object love, unmistakeably reveals its former nature. This primary narcissism recapitulated in parental love, is the equivalent to the maternal love that astonished me, with the mothers I observed in the slums of Edinburgh when I was a young midwife. This love, according to Freud, is childish. Maybe so, but it is also the opposite of being selfish.

Primary narcissism is where the child says, 'I love you and I love me'. And there is no distinction between the self and the object. In the game with the doll on the beach in *The Lost Daughter*, Elena and Nina are both playing in a creative way, with each other and with the doll. All three are versions of each other. Even their names overlap, with the girl Elena (Lenu), the mother Nina and the doll Nani, Nena or Nenella. In this game it's not just Elena, the little girl who is using the doll as a transitional object to re-find; or recreate her mother. Nina is also playing and joining in, it is a scene of mutual intimacy. As Leda watches the mother and daughter, she notices that the little girl seems 'off' in some way. As if she has been suffering from illness or saddened by a silent experience. The little girl's face turns as a silent entreaty to her mother, her expression pleading with her mother that they remain together. Leda once again observes the tenderness of the mother and the unhurried pleasure the mother and daughter both take with each other in the water. The mother spreading sun cream on her daughter's skin and hugging her, the child intertwined in the embrace with her arms wound round her mother's neck (Ferrante, 2021, p. 19).

Repairing, the lack, hurt, the loss of power, the child has experienced, Nina spoils her daughter, through the attention she provides and the game she reciprocates. Reminiscing about his 'student symbolism', Winnicott remarks that the sea is the mother which 'spews' the child onto the seashore of the mother's body, upon which the child plays (Winnicott, 2005, p. 129). This transitional experience, between mother and child, which for Nina and Elena is facilitated by the doll, is where, for Winnicott, our cultural experience is located. Cultural experience, in Winnicott's view, is an extension of transitional play and space, it links us to a 'common pool of humanity' and back to inherited tradition, our ancestors. And so transitional space is also analytic space which is constantly being reframed between our past and our future. Only this transitional play can mediate the pain that loss of omnipotence brings. No stark separations thus exist for the child in Winnicott's thinking. And perhaps this is why he ignores, rather than refuses Lacan's location of culture, and hope for the 'subject' as a linguistic cut-through with the Symbolic phallus. Equally, there is no revenge to be had with the cotton reel game and its solitary victory into language and selfhood. Primary narcissism isn't abandoned along with the mother's body, in Winnicott's story. For Winnicott, culture begins on the seashore of the mother's body onto which children are born. This beach or shore remains the ground where hope is ongoingly moved, disillusioned and remade again in increasingly wider circles. Circles for Winnicott that never cease to overlap.

If we are to think about how this sort of hope could serve at our current time, for our immediate purposes. We could imagine a hope that is realistically disillusioned and ready to discard the politics of the market and the last twenty years of so called 'economic growth'. Gains which in actuality just mean more riches for the rich, and less for the poor. But what would this more realistic hope be? Raymond Williams, in his clearsighted essay *Walking Backwards into The Future*, argues that capitalism has always aligned itself with the idea of progress. And that socialism can't pretend anymore that progress ends poverty. There is no such utopian or simple end in sight. But he does encourage us to look back at the earlier understanding of the term, socialism, which meant both society and sharing. For Williams, this is not a sharing based on what he calls the 'jingles' of consumption:

> It draws its strength from an idea of fairness, or more traditionally charity, in the distribution of what has been produced ... Neither what is called a welfare state on its own, nor what are called aid and charity to the Third World begin to measure up to the real

challenge of sharing. It is at a much earlier stage, where in certain specific ways the work has to be done, responsibility taken, care given, that the need for sharing really arises.

(Williams, 1989, p. 78)

Sharing starts early, but for it to work it has to be a pleasure, not a sacrifice. A joining in of what we want to do, as opposed to some kind of guilty reparation. In their book *Intimacies*. Leo Bersani and Adam Phillips, rework the concept of primary narcissism to elaborate their different tales of sharing. The non-personal intimacy of an analytic session, the sharing of masochistic sex between gay men, or the early sensual tie between mother and child. A sharing, which of course takes us back to the doll game on the beach, between Nina and Elena. The early narcissism that Bersani and Phillips re-describe is 'impersonal', and what they mean by that is a narcissism that is at odds with the progress story of the self and the personal ego in psychoanalysis. Impersonal narcissism is an intimacy between people, 'an experience of exchange, of intimacy, of desire indifferent to personal identity' (Bersani and Phillips, 2008, p. 122).

This description of impersonal intimacy reminds me of being in hospital recently with a lung infection. I periodically go into hospital when I suffer bouts of pneumonia, which is not uncommon with my kind of lung disease. Over the last few years, I've seen the nationality of the nurses changing. Before Brexit the hospital in Brighton was staffed with nurses from many different cultural backgrounds. Europeans made a majority of the mix, with nurses coming from France, Italy, Spain, Poland, etc. During my visit in 2023 I realised that the milieu had changed, with the majority of nurses re-locating from different parts of India, Pakistan, Bangladesh, Africa and Cuba. Nearly all of the nurses I've encountered in recent years have been wonderful, but the ones I met during my last visit were capable, kind in a way that really struck me. Despite how overworked they were, their care and professionalism remained unstinted. I talked to them about the strikes, and their pay, much of it being sent home to their families. Most of them worked on their days off to make ends meet. They were angry about the lack of pay, but it didn't interfere with their kindness or their professional expertise. One nurse I talked to said, 'nursing is natural for us, it's just an extension of what we do for our community and family at home, so it's not so different, really, doing it here'. Another nurse said:

One thing that worries me and my friends, is that we can see how individualistic life in the UK is, and we can also see how catching it might be, the lure of becoming like that. We don't want to become so tempted, that we suddenly stop wanting to look after are relatives. It horrifies us that in England you all put your parents in these terrible old people homes.

I don't doubt that many people from many different cultures experience looking after their family and community as onerous and sacrificial. And psychoanalysis has made a religion out of the necessity of leaving home as a basic premise for a happy adult life. Perhaps one of the stories in psychoanalysis that has been privileged over all the others is the story of individual separation, especially from the mother. And yet psychological individuation from the mother, doesn't have to mean that caring and closeness are then dumped. Dependency on parents goes on in today's families, well into adulthood, until it suddenly swerves into being the other way round.

The nurses helped initiate a form of impersonal intimacy with their patients, and with me, which was affectionate and caring, but it wasn't about getting to know each other in any personal way. It was a routine of practical help attached to emotional kindness which I depended on more thoroughly, and with more relief, than with my family and friends whom I tended to be more upbeat with. One of things that's always drawn me more to Winnicott than say Lacan or Klein was his refusal to demonise dependency or need. For him, it was the basis of our aliveness, our desire and joy, and it wasn't something that we should just grow out of. On the contrary it was the basis of our intimacy with each other and our creative hope. Freud didn't dwell so much on mothers or our dependence on them; but maybe that's because he took so much of his own dependency for granted. His wife, Martha, seems to have been an almost unbelievably happy character who devoted her entire life to looking after Freud. She looked after all his kids, made all his meals, was obsessed with keeping everything clean. She even organised all his travel arrangements without ever trying to interfere with his work! By all accounts she was cheerful and contented. Maybe Freud's creative life, his work, owes more to this happy dependency than has been routinely acknowledged.

What would walking backwards to a more caring society look like for us? If we are to envisage a more realistic hope, we can't really afford to ignore this question. Clearly, we could pay and value nurses and care workers more and pay mothers by instituting free child-care. But if we don't want to leave all the caring to women and migrants, then we need to start imagining what an economy of care for our society would look like. Of course, one answer to William's metaphor is that we have walked backwards too far, in a shameful fashion to the poor laws land of the nineteenth century. As Danny Dorling (2023) has suggested, 'nostalgia can be a sedative', we can't use it as an excuse for disavowing the collapse and failure of our current British state. In his remarkable and prescient book *Shattered Nation*, Dorling cites the Beveridge Report in 1942 and the plan then to remedy the five evils, want, squalor, idleness, ignorance and disease. Redescribing these evils, Dorling shows how they have been transformed today into hunger, precarity, waste, exploitation and fear. In this necessary book Dorling sketches the terrible disillusion and division that has crept up on us since the advent of Austerity in 2010. Suggesting, we might be at a turning point, Dorling emphasises this situation is not because of any utopian fantasies. It's because the levels of inequality and deprivation have become so unsustainable, they can no longer be ignored. He writes,

> We can choose now either to cultivate hope, so that we have the energy to persevere, or to burn out in exhaustion at the collective trauma that the shattering induces, and allow those who have divided us continue to do so. This is the choice we face.
>
> (Dorling, 2023, p. 21)

Psychoanalysis, today, can't afford to ignore the cultural society in which it practices. The location of culture, as Winnicott reminds us, is everywhere, inside and outside us. Hope, as Dorling says is a choice and perhaps a risk. Cynicism is much safer. And yet, we should be careful in the methods with which we hope, they should be pragmatic and agile. We can't rely on the mother of hope in any traditional sense as a religious faith, in the form of an idealised woman or saint. The mother of hope, in the different sense I have been trying to map in this paper, is something that moves, between what we can creatively imagine and the more disappointing reality we find. Hope isn't something that can remain a private fantasy, rather it's an object that has to be shared, given up and remade. It will often be broken. And then, we need to find ways of rebuilding that trust in the face of what also feels at times, a devastating loss. So, hope must keep up its companionship with other feelings such as grief, disappointment, even rage. It can't override the reality of what is actually in front of us. The harsh truth, of what the world outside currently appears to be. Reality is often brutal, but it's also the only place we find real nourishment. Thus, we need to imagine hope in the context of its only practical realisation which is in our sharing and affinity with other people. Caring, disappears, in individualistic cultures, and we need to start imagining and practicing this care, personally and impersonally in relation to our family, friends, colleagues, and community. But as I've said we can't just leave it to mothers, or carers to show up, or show us the way. We need an economy of care that is instituted at state level. A functioning welfare state is one example; one that addresses the five evils that Dorling describes. The idea that our current welfare state is too generous, or unaffordable is simply laughable. A symptom, perhaps, of the deep malaise we are all in.

Another, aspect of care we need to imagine is the realisation that it is not self-depriving, to act, in relation to climate change. On the contrary such action is a selfishly good and life preserving reality. And, when it comes to mental health, we need to acknowledge there is no longer any real state provision. That's a very grim reality. Care only works, for the mentally ill (which is all of us), like Nina and Elena's game on the beach, when it's a pleasure for both parties. Therapy, therefore, has to arguably be a pleasure as well as an urgent demand between the couple practising it. As long as we see care as a chore, whether that's for mothers, nurses or therapists, it simply won't work. Sacrifice kills pleasure, but it also turns care into a masochistic enterprise. And it doesn't have to be like that. So, if we want to creatively find some realistic hope, today, in moving forward, we need to reimagine how we care. Not as something that depletes us, but as a form of play that moves between an attention to the seriousness of the traumatic hurt, and on towards what can be creatively and practically found. In that discovery, there can be no conversions to a mother of hope that redeems us, merely one that begins again with possibilities.

References

Aquinas, T. (1966) *Summa Theologiae*, vol. 33, London, Eyre and Spottiswoode.

Bersani, L. and Phillips, A. (2008) *Intimacies*, Chicago, IL, University of Chicago Press.

Dorling, D. (2023) *Shattered Nation*, London, Verso.

Ferrante, E. (2021) *The Lost Daughter*, London, Europa Editions.

Freeman, H. (2023) *Good Girls: A Story and Study of Anorexia*, London, 4th Estate.

Freud, S. (1914) On Narcissism, in *The Standard Edition of the Complete Psychological Works of Sigmund Freud*, volume 14, translated by J. Strachey, London, Hogarth Press.

Freud, S. (1927) The Future of an Illusion, in *The Standard Edition of the Complete Psychological Works of Sigmund Freud*, volume 21, translated by J. Strachey, London, Hogarth Press.

Irigaray, L. (1993) Gesture in Psychoanalysis, in *Sexes and Genealogies*, translated by G. C. Gill, pp. 89–104, New York, Columbia University Press.

Kristeva, J. (1986a) Stabat Mater, in *The Kristeva Reader*, edited by T. Moi, pp. 160–186, Oxford, Basil Blackwell.

Kristeva, J. (1986b) Women's Time, in *The Kristeva Reader*, edited by T. Moi, pp. 187–213, Oxford, Basil Blackwell.

Levinas, E. (1992) Ethics as First Philosophy, in *The Levinas Reader*, edited by S. Hand, pp. 75–87, Oxford, Basil Blackwell.

Marrison, M. (2023) Was Lucy Letby an Unlikely Serial Killer? To Most People, Yes – but Not Psychologists, *The Guardian*, 24 August.

Phillips, A. (2024) *Giving Up*, London, Penguin Books.

Weil, S. (2005) The Self, in *Simone Weil: an Anthology*, edited and translated by S. Miles, London, Penguin Books.

Welldon, E. V. (2002) *Mothers as Creators of Sadomasochism, in Sadomasochism: Ideas in Psychoanalysis*, London, Icon Books.

Welldon, E. V. (1988) *Mother, Madonna, Whore: The Idealisation and Denigration of Motherhood*, London, Free Association Books.

Williams, R. (1989) Walking Backwards into the Future, in *Resources of Hope*, London, Verso Books.

Winnicott, D. W. (2016a) Additional Note on Psycho-Somatic Disorder, 6th September 1969, in *The Collected Works of D. W. Winnicott*, vol. 9, edited by L. Caldwell and H. T. Robinson, Oxford, Oxford University Press.

Winnicott, D. W. (2016b) Delinquency as a Sign of Hope, in *The Collected Works of D.W Winnicott*, vol. 8, edited by L. Caldwell and H. T. Robinson, Oxford, Oxford University Press.

Winnicott, D. W. (2005) *Playing and Reality*, Abingdon, Routledge.

Winnicott, D. W. (1990) *The Threat to Freedom in Home is Where We Start From*, compiled and edited by C. Winnicott, R. Shepherd and M. Davis, London, Penguin Books.

5 Nobody Knows

Illness, for Susan Sontag, means occupying the dark night of life, and once there, we hold 'a more onerous citizenship'. We all have what she calls a double citizenship, in the countries of the well and the sick. And although we all only want access to the good passport to the kingdom of the well, it is inevitable that we will eventually become residents of 'that other place' (Sontag, 2002, p. 3). Emigration, as Sontag would say to 'the kingdom of the ill', is most unbearable when it becomes mixed up with metaphor. The healthiest way to be ill, in other words, is to be the most immune to metaphors, which figure or represent that illness. However, with myalgic encephalomyelitis (ME) or chronic fatigue syndrome (CFS), it is worse than this because the metaphorical thinking that frames this disease has been historically designed to gaslight (mainly women) as suffering from hysteria. So, the metaphors of ME don't just hurt or stereotype the sufferer, they completely change it from a severe physical illness to a made up and imagined one. Imagine being really sick with cancer and going to a hospital doctor, only to be told to buck up, that there is nothing wrong with you, it's a conversion symptom! It would be inhumane, but that is exactly how our psychiatric and medical doctors, and unfortunately many therapists, have framed this illness, and this is exactly, until very recently, what they have communicated to their extremely sick patients.

When ME/CFS strikes you, life stops. The world you have been inhabiting comes to an end and you are homeless, outside of the orbit you have inhabited. You lose your job, your community, your mind, your balance, your ability to think or read, or sleep, or hold a conversation. Sometimes, as in my case, you also lose the ability to eat most things without making yourself really, sick. And the people suffering become treated as pariahs, just in the same way that AIDS victims once were, they are disrespected and humiliated by medical doctors and psychiatrists alike who think they are mad; they are abandoned by many people

DOI: 10.4324/9781003515777-5

they know who disappear into the mist. As with all serious illness that is difficult to understand or see, there is a fear of contagion and even for the people who get a sense of just how ill ME/CFS sufferers really are, people can't bear an illness that makes you so sick you can't climb out of bed, or even answer a telephone call. And ME/CFS doesn't just last a few months, it's years and years, sometimes it strikes in someone's late teens and early twenties, and they have it for a lifetime. In 2024 we learned, courtesy of Channel 4 news, the harrowing account of two families who lost their daughters in their early and late twenties. The young women had been sick for many years. It was important to the families that ME was declared on the death certificates as the reason for their deaths. How then can you describe this illness and the effect, the toll it takes on people, living a half-dead life, or indeed living in the aftermath of the children they have lost? What language can speak this or meet it. And can the body which suffers so much pain, ever actually occupy a place within language to express itself? As Elaine Scarry describes in her remarkable book *The Body in Pain*, when it comes to bodily pain, we can feel the sensation, but we can't represent it, for the ill body there is no referent or object.

> Though the capacity to experience physical pain is as primal a fact about a human being as is the capacity to hear, to touch, to desire, to fear, to hunger, it differs from these events, and from every other bodily and psychic event, by not having an object in the external world.
>
> (Scarry, 1987, p. 161)

This makes bodily pain hard to objectify and represent within language, where there is certainty for the sufferer there is doubt for the observer. Indeed, as Scarry argues physical pain has the ability, to 'shatter' language and destroy it. Unlike physical pain, psychological pain is difficult to express, although it can be and that is where psychoanalysis and psychotherapy finds its use and place. ME/CFS, however, is not psychological and is characterised by a lot of actual physical pain. Along with its myriad of symptoms, there is a complete absence of life, or energy, to perform sometimes the most basic requirements of daily life like washing, talking or eating. ME/CFS patients are too exhausted even to sleep and refreshing rejuvenating night-time rest is often diminished or lost. But there is another sense that ME/CFS is beyond language and therefore literature, and that is because people are too sick to write about their illness. And then this illness and its history becomes written up by the authorities, in the guise of the psychiatrist Simon Wessely, as a psychological complaint. Thus, this illness remains the subject of a cultural amnesia, beyond the language and power of the very subjects that need to write its story. To their dismay these patients become wrongly scribed and inscribed into a narrative that persecutes its victims every bit as much as Aids did to the gay community in the 1980s. Although ME/CFS as an illness of pain and suffering has been almost impossible to represent within language, it has repeatedly been misrepresented as hypochondria, hysteria or yuppie flu. Mocked, pitied, feared or seen as mad, ME/CFS has existed with no form inside a form and metaphor of hate and depersonalisation that obliterates the suffering of individuals concerned. In their place we find 'hystories' written by the self-named 'hystorians' that categorise ME/CFS as an imaginary melodrama and reduce it to sub-human stereotypes with no true name.

Anybody who has ever suffered from moderate to severe ME will know without having to think five minutes about it, whether they have had it for one year or forty years, that it is simply amazing that more people don't just kill themselves, because the suffering is intolerable. It is a wonder that people can struggle on with being this sick for years and years and not be completely and masochistically destroyed by it. To write about ME for the sufferer is almost impossible. Firstly, because you are too sick; people with ME are often too sick to be able to read, let alone write. And secondly, because this illness generates so much rage inside the sufferer. With cancer the illness is seen as an invader; an intruder we must fight. A list of famous women who have famously documented their breast cancer: Susan Sontag, Audre Lorde, Kathy Acker, Eve Kosofsky Sedgwick and, in the nineteenth century, Alice James, to name but a few. Breast cancer, as Eve Kosofsky Sedgwick notes, defines one's sexuality: 'Shit, now I guess I really must be a woman' (Sedgwick, 2006, p. 26) As Anne Boyer has written, there is a voluminous form to breast cancer, both written and unwritten, she suggests that 'Breast cancer is a disease that presents itself as a disordering question of form' (Boyer, 2019, p. 7). I want to explore this question of disordered form in relation to ME/CFS because with breast cancer there is an object on the X-ray, the undisputable 'granite in my breast' that Alice James describes. But with ME/CFS there is no lump of rock, or granite, no material entity that can diagnosed on a scan or screen. Instead, there is a long history of hysteria or silence, the horror of raw affects without any form whatsoever to give a shape to the person's anguish and distress.

Before Alice James suffered, and died, from breast cancer, she endured a lifetime of neurasthenia, or what was named hysteria – illness of the nerves. Neurasthenia is inseparable today from a description of ME. As a psychoanalyst and a literary critic who once worked in academia I've been well versed in the narratives of hysteria and literary criticism. I've even taught Elaine Showalter's book *Hystories* (1998), and to my shame, could not see then the damage it did. I had been taught about hysteria and obsession as neurotic symptoms in my psychoanalytic training and this was before my illness started so I bought into the hysteria myth of women's illness that continues to this day. In her book Showalter lists the six so-called psychogenic syndromes of the 1990s: 'chronic fatigue, Gulf War syndrome, multiple personality disorder, recovered memory of sexual abuse, satanic ritual abuse and alien abduction'. Continuing, she explains that 'The histories of these syndromes are linked and overlapping … all these syndromes move towards suspicion, conspiracy theories, witch-hunts, and mass panics.' Wanting to distinguish between 'metaphors and realities' and between therapeutic narratives and 'destructive hystories' Showalter invites us to see hysteria, not as a disease but as 'protolanguage'. Although Showalter knew nothing about ME/CFS as a real illness, like her comrade in arms the psychiatrist Simon Wessely, she circulated the now widely believed crackpot mantra that this illness is made up of purely imaginary symptoms. Like Wessely, Showalter uses the history of neurasthenia as a pipeline connecting nineteenth-century so-called hysterics with modern-day sufferers of ME/CFS. The modern-day hysterics like me, with CFS, refuse to believe we are really psychologically ill:

> Spurning the idea they can be helped with psychotherapy and anti-depressants, chronic fatigue patients might go on for a few years, becoming more and more invested in the fruitless quest for a medical breakthrough.
>
> (Showalter, 1998, p. 129)

Showalter cites the 'hystory' of hysteria, tracing it back to Freud and Charcot. Whereas Charcot saw hysteria as a unified organise disease, Freud understood it as the repression of internal sexual conflict. Histories of psychoanalytic feminism have indeed seen hysteria and feminism as twinned, with John Forrester and Lisa Appignanesi arguing in *Freud's Women* that the social purity and asceticism of nineteenth-century movements like temperance or hygiene, and the fixed ideals they aspired to, could explain middle-class women's repression of sexuality and desires and their hysterical symptoms (Appignanesi and Forrester, 2005). And of course, this is very true, but the repression of desire, for Freud's female hysterics, was the internal conflict generated by both psychic and social prohibitions. It had nothing to do with women being biomedically ill, even if hysterical symptoms were played out and converted onto the body. I will come back to this later as the whole concept of

desire is in question if you are too sick to move or function. It's like imagining making love or having sex with someone if you have raging flu, the
whole question of female desire and hysteria has to be revisited once we
understand the woman's hysterical body as really sick ... If hysteria in
Freud's today was an illness of its historical time, rather than some timeless
and universal idea, then we have to be extremely careful of ascribing
someone's physically ill symptoms to a psychological condition.

Freud himself became a victim of the 'hysteria myth' by his biographer
Ernest Jones, who attributed his intermittent angina and palpitations to
'hysterical anxiety'. Whereas Freud's own GP in later life, Dr Schur,
disagreed and was convinced Freud had suffered a previous coronary as a
younger man, with subsequent bouts of angina being brought on by
smoking. Freud's more serious physical illness, his oral cancer, was
something he described as 'torture'. Nicholas Lazaridis, a professor of
oral and maxillofacial surgery in Greece, has documented the tortuous
journey of mouth cancer Freud underwent for 16 years from 1923 to
when it eventually killed him in 1939. Freud, initially diagnosed in April
1923, by his family physician Felix Deutsch and his friend Maxim Steiner, was not told the truth at the time that he suffered from advanced
squamous cell cancer. To 'spare' his feelings they minimised the cancer
in his right posterior hard palate. They told him that his lesions were a
'bad case of leucoplakia due to excessive smoking'. Freud, not believing
them, of course, referred to the pain in his mouth as 'my dear neoplasm'
(Lazaridis, 2003, p. 78). Angry at his doctor's refusal to tell him the truth
and refusing to see Deutsch for months, Freud sought out the help of a
professor of laryngology, a Markus Hajek. In Freud's memoirs, Schur
mentions how unqualified Hajek was, and clearly not up to the job.
Going into detail, with the insight of time and experience behind him,
Lazaradis is blunter. He states the operation was a 'botch' (Lazaridis,
2003, p. 79). Hajek did not remove all of the tumour, and left Freud to
bleed out in his clinic overnight, with a haemorrhage, unattended by any
medical staff. Freud was unable to cry for help and was found bloodied
and dazed by his daughter Anna, who then refused to leave his side.
Later in the year, in September, Deutsch accompanied Freud to a more
competent surgeon, Hans Pichler. Pichler went on to oversee many
operations on Freud's mouth over the subsequent months and years.
When too much tissue had been removed Pichler famously made the
'objurator prosthesis', or the 'evil necessity; a device inserted into
Freud's mouth, enabling him to eat and speak'. Freud dubbed it 'the
monster' (Lazaradis, 2003, p. 81). Freud's suffering was indeed very
great, and in 1936, shortly after another surgery was completed, more
calamity occurred, when the Nazis entered Vienna. Anna became

arrested and although she was released, this was the warning that the family heeded before their flight to the UK. Professor Pichler was one of the people who helped Freud escape. Freud's personal resilience and hope in the last sixteen years of his life are impressive. It's also interesting that his physical suffering and illness have received so little attention. Ernest Jones was not the only follower of Freud to make a psychosomatic analysis of his real illness. Wilhelm Reich linked his jaw cancer to Freud's character armour, his repressed sexuality. In fact, so convinced was Reich by his theories that he made sexual release and orgone therapy the cure for not just neurosis but physical disorders too. As if having more sex would cure Freud's mouth cancer! And yet releasing trauma through the body has become something of a renaissance in current times, as if trauma is an imprisoned bodily energy we can transform through sex, or even intense emotional release.

Given that illness attracts metaphors so strongly, possibly due to the horror and fear invoked by the literal symptoms of severe illness and disease, why consign ME to the out of date, woman blaming myth of hysteria? Metaphors are inextricable from thinking, but they are not innocent things. Metaphors can hurt and in the case of ME as we will see, they can also kill. As a myth, hysteria has attached itself since Freud's day, to repressed sexuality, war trauma, and to any expression of an excess of emotion or feeling. This myth has been used by some of our top psychiatrists to demonise ME, and is a stark warning that the hysteria myth will also start to frame sufferers of long COVID too. In fact, that demonisation has already begun; something which I will return to later. So, given that ME is going to attract metaphors, we can't think about it without them, how about giving it one that is more intelligent and imaginative; one that contains compassion for the real physical pain and bodily deterioration of the sufferer?

I will continue with rather an absurd, but I think truer, metaphor for ME, Kafka's *Metamorphosis*. In this famous novella, Gregor, a travelling salesman, wakes up one morning to find he has been transformed into a monstrous beetle or cockroach. Finding it difficult to walk or use his feeble legs, his first dilemma is how to make it out of the bed. He is weak and rooted by the broad shell of his back to lying helplessly watching his tiny legs flail helplessly:

> However violently he forced himself to his right side he always rolled over onto his back again. He tried it at least a hundred times, shutting his eyes to keep from seeing his struggling legs, and only desisted when he began to feel in his side a faint dull ache he had never experienced before.
>
> (Kafka, 1988, p. 94)

Gregor's sudden transformation is not unlike the metamorphosis that overtakes patients with ME. Gregor can't get out of bed, he can't sleep and eventually can't eat anything either. Kafka wrote to Max Brod in 1915 insisting that the cockroach in his story must not appear on the front cover: 'The insect is not to be drawn. It is not even to be seen from a distance' (Kafka, 2016, p. 52). The monstrous beetle wasn't literal; it was a metaphor of dehumanisation. Kafka wanted the reader to imagine the form of the cockroach. It was a deliberately hazy image of a person's alienation, and it works to symbolise that estrangement. In the story Gregor's life before he wakes up in the country of the ill, was to work very hard as a travelling salesman supporting both his parents and sister. The family are horrified when they witness Gregor's sudden change into a giant insect. The mother insists he is ill but can't look at him and screams and faints in his presence: seeing him sickens her. The father is furious, pushing Gregor back into his bedroom with his walking stick, damaging one side of Gregor's body in the process. In another tantrum the father pelts Gregor with apples, with one becoming lodged into his back and really hurting him. Only the sister has compassion, removing the furniture in his room so Gregor can run about on the walls or hang from the ceiling. But over time she too becomes disgusted and indifferent to Gregor's plight.

The families of ME patients are very different and often they are the only people who look after sufferers, working often as unpaid carers. The family in *Metamorphosis*, however, are not kind and they are part of the community that continues Gregor's dehumanisation, deliberately, or by just ignoring his monstrous symptoms. Mostly they are simply aghast, and yet as time goes on, they seem to puff up and flourish in their rejection of Gregor, as though he represents everything they can't bear about themselves. Thus, they leave him to rot in his room. Gregor eventually gives up and dies, from neglect and lack of food and care. Gregor's family represent the state infrastructures that are meant to care for ME patients and yet have remained judgemental, incurious and indifferent. The NHS, the DWP, the psychologists, particularly of the infamous PACE trial, which for many years informed the psychological definition and treatment of ME patients. Depriving them of necessary disability benefits, but also preventing proper research and funding into a medical illness. The PACE trial has been rescinded after the methodology was found universally by scientists to be faulty and, in many people's view fraudulent.

The expectation in *Metamorphosis* that Gregor works despite his new debilitating transformation is exemplified by his employer, the chief clerk, who shows up at his house, the minute its apparent Gregor has missed the early train to work, to berate him:

Here you are ... causing your parents a lot of unnecessary trouble
and ... neglecting your business duties in an incredible fashion ...
You amaze me, I thought you were a quiet dependable person and
all at once you seem bent on making a disgraceful exhibition of
yourself.

(Kafka, 1988, p. 97)

Like the ME patients who are deemed fit to work when they are often
unable to get out of bed, Gregor is disbelieved by his employer, who
thinks he is malingering and hysterical. Kafka, himself, much like Freud
suffered for many years with illness. Diagnosed in 1917 with TB, Kafka
was pensioned off from his job and spent his remaining life in various
sanitoriums. The year of his diagnosis in 1917, Kafka writes to his friend
Max Brod, telling him:

You ask about my illness ... True, I am short of breath but don't
feel it when lying or sitting, and while I am walking or doing any
work, I manage by breathing twice as quickly as previously, no great
hardship. I've come to think that tuberculosis is no special disease,
or not a disease that needs a special name, but only the germ of
death itself, intensified.

(Kafka, 2016, p. 151)

Metamorphosis has been given many meanings over the years, through
Marxism or Existentialism to describe exploitation by capitalism, or
alienation by society. Kafka wrote *Metamorphosis* just before he got
sick, but maybe there was a premonition or early symptoms, as in the
story, Gregor's beetle status confers on him, breathlessness and less
than dependable lungs. Kafka's novella signifies the monstrous illness
of ME, precisely because of the inhumane way patients are treated by
the very institutions who are supposed to care for them. Today, as we
move into an age of COVID-19, we are beginning to see a tsunami of
long COVID, which are really the sister symptoms to ME/CFS. It is
perhaps only now that the full horror of this illness will receive the
attention and funding it so deserves. MECFS is a complex illness of the
immune system. An active inflammation of all systems of the body,
stemming from inflammation of the brain and spinal-cord and caused
by active viral infection. There are reduced intestinal barriers, and an
uneven ratio of too many bad bugs in the gut which causes ongoing
inflammation in the bowel as well as other systems in the body. ME/
CFS. is a vast system of subgroups, and symptoms are multiple and
varied, muscle and nerve pain, brain fog, fibromyalgia, headaches,

allergies, hives, hormone problems, problems with digestion, extreme diarrhoea, unrefreshing sleep, sore throats, fevers, heart palpitations, dysautonomia and orthostatic intolerance.

A professor of clinical immunology in the USA, Nancy Klimas has divided her clinical career between treating HIV patients and those suffering from ME/CFS. In 2009 she writes about how her HIV patients are, on the whole, 'hale and hearty' because of decades of research and funding that have brought about successful treatment and prevention. In comparison, ME patients are 'terribly sick' and not able to function either at work or within their families. 'If I had to choose between the two illnesses', Klimas writes, 'I would rather have HIV' (Klimas, 2015). With ME you can feel as sick as you do with late-stage cancer or HIV, but with ME, you don't as a rule die from the illness, you live but just feel like you are dying. It's literally, for anyone who cares to research it, a living death because the body simply doesn't work or function. A fellow sufferer once said to me that ME/CFS is having an addiction to life because it's such a huge act of will to try and live any semblance of a daily life. Your body wants to stay in bed and give up, but your 'self' wants to live, walk, eat, socialise and travel. Most of these things are severely limited in severe ME/CFS with extreme cases where people are literally paralysed in bed being tube fed. You are in a constant losing fight with your body. Even moderate illness means a life which is incredibly limited in terms of what you can do. Unsurprisingly, people who don't have this particular illness, don't understand the phenomena and are suspicious and frightened, which make them behave in unsympathetic ways by ignoring or minimising the illness. If you think this is an exaggeration, just ask anyone who has suffered or anyone who has been a long-term carer for an ME sufferer in their family. Most ME sufferers are very angry about their illness, not, as our chief psychiatrist Simon Wessely opines, because they are all hysterics, languishing in bed, but precisely because their anger is a sign of their spirit, the evidence that they have not completely given up. ME is the biggest medical scandal of the twentieth and twenty-first century because it has been ignored, trivialised, gaslighted, and seen as a modern psychosomatic form of neurasthenia belonging particularly to women. The terror of this illness for everybody is its invisibility. The sufferers look normal, blood tests come back relatively normal, as the wrong things are being tested. Doctors are taught not to see it, in medical school students are still taught it's a psychiatric condition. GPs don't want to see it, as testing wastes resources, and even if they realise the very real physical illness presenting, its beyond their medical knowledge to treat. One GP once told me, pulsing with impatience, under her breath, to 'get a life'. I had just got sick and couldn't walk or lift a hairbrush or read. I couldn't climb the stairs or load the dishwasher. I was so weak I thought I was either dying, or mad because no-one except the people that loved me were taking any notice. My legs were numb, I had terrible chest pain, hive-like rashes on my face and body, migraines, constant diarrhoea and a BP that would suddenly accelerate into frightening high numbers along with palpitations that would send me zooming into hospital in an ambulance. Once there they would find nothing in my blood, and I was merely told it was anxiety or an allergy. Another GP said to me on a first visit, '97% of the people that walk through my door I can help, you are among the 3% I can't help because you have ME. I'm very sorry but I will not waste my practice's resources on tests that will just come back as negative.' At least he was honest.

ME/CFS is a disease that virtually nobody knows how either to frame or treat. If cancer is a 'disorganising question of form' then ME/CFS is the absence of any generative or recognisable form. The shape it is given is the most derogatory form of all women's illness, a fantasy one, hysteria. A psychiatric illness that is supposedly psychosomatic and sham, in that the woman is languishing in bed, suffering from yuppie flu, masquerading and making it up to get attention. Of course, all illness is psychosomatic, but we can never know what the psychological triggers and consequences of any illness really are. But just as we would think it both overly crude, ridiculous and cruel to reduce someone's cancer to their marriage breakdown or depression, so it is similarly perverse to pathologise ME/CFS as psychological because we can't medically fully understand let alone treat it. I remember saying this in a seminar I convened on psychoanalysis and creativity at Kings College years ago (when I was well enough to travel to London). A young male PhD student answered me by disagreeing. 'But there is obvious psychosomatic illness like ME and you wouldn't call childhood leukaemia psychosomatic, would you?' I think back and want that moment over again, so I can give a better answer. What I would say is now that they are completely the same with respect to being psychosomatic; just as trauma might trigger the immune system into not responding well enough to the viruses that cause ME/CFS so we just can't know what stress has evolved in a child or his family, that might trigger a cancer. The mind and body are not separate, at least I can't envisage a disembodied brain, but I also know that however well connected they are, the body has a secret life all of its own.

Everybody is terrified of too much uncertainty, the absence of a form to represent our experience and our suffering. Consequently, everybody becomes terrified of the illness with no form, no categorisation and no name. Doctors are frightened of it because it largely defies current medical knowledge, friends and family find it hard to bear because the person they love disappears and is replaced by a human bundle of pain and misery who often can't function on any level. Other people look on in horror at the absolute helplessness involved in an individual that can look relatively well but be unable to perform the simplest task. Their inability to understand can make them both frightened and judgemental. Thus, there is cultural amnesia of this illness and disavowal on just about every level. The recipients of the disease are both frightened and scapegoated, and they learn pretty quickly to shut up and stay silent about their symptoms. Writing now, by definition, I am not so sick as I was, although my ME has migrated to different inflammatory diseases of my lung. So, I regularly have pneumonia and am hospitalised and despite the anxiety involved, all the intravenous antibiotics have seemed to help my ME symptoms, especially my gut. I can work part-time, and have my social and personal life back, even if there are always limits on how well I can be. Living with disability has changed me, in many ways for the better. I am a better therapist, and far more present to my client's vulnerability, because it no longer stands in for my own. I even understand people's reaction to this illness. How could I not as I used to share, in part, the same stereotypes?

Nobody knows what this illness is, or how to treat it or how sick it makes people and because of such uncertainty everyone is very frightened. The ME sufferer gets accused of malingering or being an hysteric or making it up. Sir Simon Wessely is our chief psychiatrist in the UK and chief minimiser of ME/CFS as a credible illness. We could call him our 'chief clerk'. He has long argued for the psychological aetiology of this disease, as though it's just a form of hysteria we can recover from. Arguing that CFS is not an immunodeficiency caused by viral infection; without a scrap of evidence to back this up, Wessely continues to wonder whether the ongoing fatigue is just a modern version of eighteenth-century neurasthenia. Where patients who might have once had a virus but are just now avoiding the activity for getting better. At the beginning of my illness, I was in a great deal of denial of what was happening to me, it was before my diagnosis, and I forced myself out one day on my shaky legs, to meet an academic friend for a drink. We were talking about her research into fatigue, and she told me in conversation about her colleague Simon Wessely who was being sent death threats by ME/CFS patients and how awful it was. And I remember saying, or at least thinking, at the time, but why would they do that, what if these people are really ill? That conversation with my friend in a pub still comes back to haunt me, fourteen years later, as if I knew then, so early on, what was wrong with me, but couldn't let myself believe it.

Looking at what Simon Wessely has written about CFS patients is informative.

Assessing the anger of CFS patients to psychiatrists and doctors, Wessely used it as further evidence of their over-emotionality and their inability to distinguish physical symptoms from psychological ones:

> The often intense dislike and distrust of psychiatry is well attested in the now voluminous self-help literature. In the professional literature, CFS patients have been described as resentful and hostile towards psychiatrists ... or even towards all doctors. Stewart (in press) concludes that these patients view psychological difficulties as weaknesses, and such diagnosis leads to anger and resentment. Clinically, this may result in a marked dissociation between the perception of physical and psychological symptoms in fatigued patients ...
>
> (Wessely, 1990, p. 90)

Reading this, how can we fail to see the legitimate truth of the anger that many ME/CFS patients have felt towards psychiatrists, specifically Simon Wessely, who was repeatedly sent death threats by some CFS sufferers? We have to ask: why would patients so sick they can't get out of bed rise up with assassination threats against a psychiatrist? When you actually grasp the enormous damage Wessely has singlehandedly dished out to the ME/CFS community, maybe the anger is more understandable; not because these people are mad or emotionally unstable, but because they are victims of stigmatisation by the medical community. Because of Wessely and his colleagues' classification of CFS as a psychosomatic form of neurasthenia and psychiatric disorder, the official treatment offered for this illness under the NICE guidelines, until the rescinding of the PACE trial, were psychological and behavioural. Recommended protocols were cognitive behavioural therapy and graded exercise to reverse the deconditioning (of the patient languishing in bed). Psychological therapy for CFS is useless to remedy any symptoms, or its as useful as giving psychotherapy to cancer patients would be in treating their tumours. And graded exercise is positively dangerous as making CFS patients do more exercise makes them much sicker. Moreover, the psychological nature of the NICE guidelines has made it impossible for ME/CFS patients to receive the disabled benefits they should be entitled to. This makes gaining benefits for being unable to work, obtaining home help or getting disabled car parking virtually impossible. In fact, most disabled benefits are still withheld from ME/CFS patients as they are deemed too able to warrant them.

Perhaps, listening to some of Wessely's categorisation of ME as psychosomatic, will clarify some of the individual sufferer's rage. Earlier in his career, in a chapter called 'Chronic Fatigue and Myalgia Syndromes', Wessely remarks, 'Most CFS patients fulfil diagnostic criteria for psychiatric disorder' (Wessely, 1990, p. 82). Noting that hospital patients cite infection as the initial cause of their fatigue, Wessely remarks that this was also the case with neurasthenia at the beginning of the 20th Century, however, he questions whether there is any justification, for 'classifying CFS by any alleged infectious or other aetiological association' (Wessely, 1990, p. 84) In the *Journal of The Royal College of General Practitioners*, Wessely and colleagues write:

> Many patients referred to a specialised hospital with chronic fatigue syndrome have embarked on a struggle. This may take the form of trying to find an acceptable diagnosis, or indeed any diagnosis. One of the principal functions of therapy at this stage is to allow the patient to call a halt without loss of face ... ME patients are in a vicious circle of increasing avoidance, inactivity and fatigue ...
>
> (Wessely et al., 1989, p. 27)

In *Chronic Fatigue and its Syndromes*, a book written jointly by Wessely and two academic psychologists, the following statements are made:

> ME/CFS/CFIDS is better understood not as a result of any unique or specific aspect of late 19th century life, but as a fin de siècle illness, just as neurasthenia was itself a fin de siècle illness of the nineteenth century ... Explanations and descriptions of ME/CFIDs are thus not always to be taken a literal truths, but as metaphorical descriptions.
>
> (Wessely, Hotopf and Sharpe, 1999, p. 338)

Imagine a psychiatrist saying that about AIDS, or cancer or COVID-19, and getting away with it. Wessely seems to explain the psychosomatic aetiology of ME as an illness that progresses because the patient's determination to find a diagnosis, any diagnosis, and their avoidance (disavowal) of the psychological aspects of their illness leads to increasing fatigue and inactivity. If there was ever a modern-day witch hunt against vulnerable patients, more often women, then this is an example. I don't wish this illness on Simon Wessely, but his work remains a stain on the history of both medical and psychiatric research. He should be stripped of his knighthood, awarded to him by the Cameron government, for his services to the ME/CFS community in 2013. As Dr Charles Shepherd, medical advisor to the ME Association, remarked in an article in the *Telegraph*:

The time has come for doctors and scientists to apologise for the very neglectful way in which ME has been researched and treated over the last 60 years. Doctors need to start listening to their patients and there must now be increased investment in biomedical research to gain a better understanding of the disease process and to develop treatments that these patients desperately need.

(Shepherd, 2015)

That apology needs to be led by our government. The shame attached to honouring Simon Wessely for helping to serve this community, when he has done more than any other individual to set back the humane treatment, care and funding of ME/CFS, is simply immeasurable. Fellow scientists opposed his award in 2012 of the John Maddox Ford Prize for bravery in facing opposition to his views about ME and Gulf War Syndrome. Professor Malcolm Hooper, a scientist whose biomedical research stands firmly behind the science for ME/CFS as disordered immunity, remarks:

Given that Wessely's belief that ME is a somatoform disorder has been comprehensively invalidated by the scientific evidence, for him to have received a prize for 'standing up for science' for his work on ME/CFS has resulted in deserved derision, not least because it does not accord with the Declaration of Helsinki: section B11 requires that 'Medical research involving human subjects must conform to generally accepted scientific principles (and) be based on a thorough knowledge of the scientific literature', but Wessely's work ignores the existing scientific literature.

(Hooper, 2012)

Follow the science has become something of a mantra, since Covid 19 has hit, but we are also seeing not just how uncertain Science really is, but how it is interpreted can vary so differently. Psychiatry has always presumed to know and to diagnose, both mental and physical symptoms that are never reducible to their classification. When you really listen to symptoms, and I don't think psychiatrists are particularly good at this, and you listen for long enough. The boundaries of the psychological illness 'lift and evaporate'. I don't think we are in much need of any more psychiatric classifications, but we badly need to really listen to people's symptoms. And perhaps start believing what patients are telling us. Just because there has been no evidence of the pain and physical distress ME patients are in, just because there might be some sort of doubt of what is occurring in the body, does not mean we should disbelieve them. But that is exactly what Wessely and his motley crew have succeeded in doing, and they have persuaded the science to follow them. If it wasn't so terrible it would be laughable.

Virginia Woolf talks about illness as the worm on the end of a hook, struggling for life. 'But with the hook of life still in us still must we wriggle' (Woolf, 2012, p.17). Woolf writes of the absence of accounts of illness in literature. Novels, she declares, concern themselves with the mind, and thus the

> body is a sheet of plain glass through which the soul looks straight and clear, and, save for one or two passions such as desire and greed, is null, negligible and non-existent. On the contrary the very opposite is true. All day, all night the body intervenes; blunts or sharpens, colours, or discolours, turns to wax in the warmth of June, hardens to tallow in the murk of February. The creature within can only gaze through the pane – smudged or rosy; it cannot separate off from the body like the sheath of a knife or the pod of a pea for a single instant; it must go through the whole unending procession of changes, heat and cold, comfort and discomfort, hunger and satisfaction, health and illness, until there comes the inevitable catastrophe; the body smashes itself to smithereens, and the soul (it is said) escapes. But of all of this daily drama of the body there is no record.
>
> (Woolf, 2012, p. 4)

As Woolf notes, a novel about illness would lack plot, indeed there is no narrative arc to writing about sickness. The poverty of language in relation to literature means that in, 'English, which can express the thoughts of Hamlet and the tragedy of Lear, has no words for the shiver and the headache. It has all grown one way.' In ME/CFS the shiver and the headache, remain not only undocumented and unseen but they are also actively denied and negated. The very doctors who are meant to read this particular body, doubt it. The symptoms that could tell the true story are written up in an English that swaps the shiver and headache, into another story where we are simply imagining these physical torments.

In *Metamorphosis*, when Gregor becomes sick (or a beetle) his voice changes to a 'horrible twittering squeak'; so much so that on hearing his words, the chief clerk backs away from him and makes for the exit. Gregor is desperate that the chief clerk stays to hear him out: 'The chief clerk must be detained, soothed, persuaded and finally won over. The future of Gregor and his family depended on it!' (Kafka, 1988, p. 102).

In a similar fashion the sufferers of ME have been dependant on the authorities who continue to scapegoat and hurt them. The chief clerk's disgust as Gregor for being disabled and his view that he is making a hysterical exhibition of himself is just like the psychologists who have disbelieved the real illness of ME and gaslighted their patients accordingly. Because the PACE trial was funded in part by DWP it was extremely effective in denying ME patients necessary disability benefits, forcing them into work, or poverty if they were too sick. More than this, it caused many patients active harm as its prescribed treatments, GET (graded exercise) has caused horrific harm to patients and of course therapy is part of the gaslighting that persuades everyone of a psychological aetiology. The PACE trial was published in 2011 by the *Lancet*, the year I became sick. The authors, influenced by our chief clerk Wessely, were Professors Peter White, Michael Sharpe and Trudie Chalder.

Carol Monaghan, a Scottish National MP, has called ME and the PACE trial the biggest medical scandal of this century. In a parliamentary debate in 2019, Monaghan relayed the shocking story of an 8-year-old girl, falling seriously sick with ME, who was not believed. Social services, referred by a psychiatrist who had initially assessed the child, put her on the at-risk register, threatening the parents with court action and arrest unless they complied with the ME treatment of graded exercise. This treatment put the child in a wheelchair, and after the parents admitted her to a specialised ME unit, thinking this would help, she was given more graded exercise, whereupon she got much sicker. The mother was banned from visiting and the family were again threatened with removing the child to a psychiatric hospital or foster care, if she did not improve. Eventually, the child returned home after many months, but the injury done was irreversible. By the age of 15 years, this girl was paralysed, bed-ridden and being tube fed. The opposition, at first for the release of the PACE trial data, was world-wide, from scientists, patients and ME organisations. Queen Mary's University refused many times to release the date. Eventually after numerous attempts, and a tribunal they were forced to. The results showed, the study was biased and seriously flawed. Today the Nice guidelines have been changed to reflect ME as the physical illness it is, but for many people the damage has been done. Moreover, plenty of therapists and doctors still believe ME is psychological. I meet plenty of them. Believing illness is hysterical or psychological is sewn into society's way of thinking about illness. As Sontag has shown, there is a long history of psychologising both TB and Cancer, in science and literature. ME is just the latest victim; it was vulnerable to being classified as hysterical precisely because medical tests show nothing, and sufferers don't always look unwell. The authors of the PACE trial have never been publicly made to retract their myth-based nonsense. On the contrary, they have all flourished, much like Gregor's family in Kafka's story, they have gone on to lead comfortable successful lives as esteemed professors, at the expense of ME sufferers. After Gregor's death from his family's neglect in *Metamorphosis*, the parents, can forget the sorrow he caused them. They find a better situated house. And become contented in the sight of their blossoming daughter, whom they agree is ready, for a fine husband, 'And it was like a confirmation of their new dreams and excellent intentions' (Kafka, 1988, p. 139).

In truth, the father in *Metamorphosis* does more harm to Gregor than simply ignoring him. Coming home one day and having found Gregor has escaped from his room, causing his mother to faint again, the father goes into another rage, bombarding Gregor with apples from the sideboard:

> [An apple] thrown without much force grazed Gregor's back and glanced off harmlessly. But another following immediately landed right on his back and sank in; Gregor wanted to drag himself forward, as if this surprising incredible pain could be left behind him, but he felt as if nailed to the spot and flattened himself out in a complete derangement of all his senses.
>
> (Kafka, 1988, p. 122)

The apples in this story symbolise both suffering and betrayal; caused, by the psychologists who instigated and perpetuated the hysterical myth that in turn produced and executed the PACE Trial. These psychologists are not just chief clerks, but also our chief apple throwers, whose apples have seriously injured the very people they claim to sympathise with and treat. One recent apple, by Michael Sharpe has recently gone so far in the delusion that long Covid is hysteria that he has accused the journalist George Monbiot, of the dangers of spreading Long Covid, by writing about it in the Guardian. And Simon Wessely, in 2015, threw another apple by defending the PACE trial as a 'thing of beauty'. Beautiful for him and his colleagues perhaps, but as a theory and practice of the hysteria myth, it has harmed and, in some cases, destroyed the health of thousands of people, perhaps especially the young and vulnerable.

I'm walking to work, it's the end of the summer term in 2011, and am struck as always by just how picturesque the campus at the University of Birmingham is. The sky is an unusually bright blue for Birmingham; a blue that reflects and bounces off the red bricks of the old historic buildings that surround the central square. Old Joe, the tall Tolkien clock tower, rises up, up above the blossoming trees with the students lying on the grass in groups or bustling to last minute assignments with tutors. The English department with leaded windows opening out between covers of thick wondrous green ivy, leaves that will fire into red, orange and yellow as autumn approaches. All academic departments have a collective character. When I was in cultural studies it was a competition to be leftist, rebellious especially to the central administration. But English, where I was left after cultural studies shut down, had no such spirit. It was a studious, sacrificial place, where obsessions over editing books and the finer details of prose took precedence over ideas, and of course over what any member of staff or student might be feeling on a day-to-day basis. I wasn't feeling well and the staff meeting which I knew would be interminable, usually focusing for hours on how we had to change the style guide for the upcoming term, filled me with dread. I thought not for the first time, how beautiful the English department was on the outside and how ugly and dispiriting on the inside; how unhappy the people that worked there actually were. Or perhaps that's untrue, perhaps they were perfectly happy, and it was me who couldn't cope with their obsessional characters, concerned only with novels of the mind, cut off like Woolf's pane of glass from their bodily emotions and experiences.

Night-time, and I am sleeping over at my mate's house, Danielle, from American studies. Woken by pain drumming in my head, I rush to the toilet, and it feels like my insides are coming out, then I vomit. Eventually I stand shakily and pass out. Sensing Danielle's presence bending over me, her pale face worried. 'Hi Jan, are you okay, shall I call a doctor?'

'No,' I said, 'I've just got a virus, holiday sickness, coming early, I'll be fine.'

But I wasn't fine, not the next day, or the next week. In fact, I don't ever recover. One and a half years later, I'm sitting in the consulting room of Patrick Gordon, who is a consultant rheumatologist at King's College Hospital. I've been driven there by my partner, as I can't walk very well. The muscles in my legs and arms are very weak, I suffer from muscle and nerve pain, I can't climb stairs without difficulty, the headaches and colitis attacks continue daily, and during the night. The shocking symptoms I first experienced at Danielle's house become a regular feature of my life. Waking up on the cream linoleum of the bathroom floor in the early hours of the morning, my partner's cradling arms under my head, looking anxiously at me and telling me I'll be fine, even though we both know I'm not. I have strange rashes and hives that come and go, spreading over my torso and face. Food intolerances mean I can't eat gluten, wheat or dairy, I've lost nearly 10 kg in weight. I'm on prednisolone, a strong steroid, and have been through a complex series of brain scans and muscle and nerve tests that have taken many months.

It's been a long road, starting at the Sussex County at Brighton where, after Crohn's disease and brain tumours were queried and ruled out, the medical staff then discharged me. I then phoned a kind gastro-enterologist, Professor Bjarnason at Kings College hospital, who listens attentively to my history.

'I don't know what's the matter with you,' he said, 'but I have no doubt whatsoever you are seriously ill. You have been without a diagnosis for too long. We are going to find out by throwing the book at you.' After many tests on my bowels and bloods, he calls me back in and says, 'I was worried you had pancreatic cancer, but you don't, and your small bowel is also clear. I'm afraid I don't know what's wrong with you, but I suspect it's autoimmune in nature. I can't help you further, so I'm referring you to my colleague Patrick in the rheumatology department.'

Initially paying for private help with Patrick, I was told that he suspected lupus, because of the inflammatory pain in my chest and numbness in my arms and legs, or dermatomyositis, a wasting disease of the muscles, because my limbs were so weak. It's been many months of tests and investigations, I'm so tired of being so sick and without a diagnosis, I'm still full of hope that whatever the results prove I will get some kind of treatment. Patrick is a really lovely man, thin slightly stooped, with an intelligent mobile face. Luckily for me he has always listened carefully and taken my symptoms very seriously. He gives me a grave smile, and says, 'I'm glad to say, as far as we can tell you don't have any of the terrible diseases we have tested you for. You do have a diffuse auto-immune illness, but in the absence of antibodies, the diagnosis is severe chronic fatigue syndrome.'

All I knew about chronic fatigue syndrome was what I had read in Elaine Showalter's book *Hystories*, and because I was a psychoanalyst, I knew it was widely understood in the therapy world as a hysterical illness. 'I can't have that,' I replied quickly. 'I'm far too ill.'

'People with this condition are and do feel very ill,' said Patrick, 'and it's the only thing that explains your ongoing symptoms in the absence of any positive test results.'

I feel stunned, this is difficult to take in. 'I have been unable to walk, or read or socialise for nearly a year,' I say, 'when will I get better?'

'With the severity of your illness and your age of 52, in my clinical experience I don't think you will ever get better,' he replied. 'Unfortunately, at this time, there is no cure for what you have. You won't be able to work as an academic anymore, I can write you a letter for medical retirement. I'm very sorry but my advice to you is to try every alternative medical approach you can.'

'I can't accept that I'm this sick and you can't help me,' I reiterated, 'I won't accept that I'm not going to get better.' He smiled again, a bit sadly. 'I'm afraid I've done what I can ...'

I return home and spend many weeks and months feeling sick and frightened. I try out various GPs, but none of them are interested; if they are, they just recommend cognitive behavioural therapy. I know the difference between depression and illness, and I feel too sick to move but desperate to get better. That's not depression, but still, I doubt myself. I ask my supervisor, Adam, 'Do you think this is hysteria?' His reply was categorical: 'No, I don't, I think you are really ill.'

I go and visit a Chinese herbalist I've been seeing for years for rhinitis. He says, 'Your immune system is overactive, that's why you have the fatigue.' I take the herbs, but I still wonder, could it be psychological? So, I embark on the Lightning Process, which is cognitive rewiring of the brain. It's a secret process, copyrighted to make money, but it actually involves walking round a square telling yourself over and over again, you are leaving the pit, and becoming a powerful genius who can do anything. I practice it over and over again, before I do any activity. I walk around in the square when I get up, after breakfast, before I open the front door to a friend or the postman. It doesn't work, but then I'm in a world where nobody knows, and no treatment works, so I figure I have nothing to lose. I'll try everything. I'll try the process again and again, I want to believe this is psychological because then there is a cure, and end in sight ... I'm a therapist, who has never had depression, but perhaps this is my body's way of telling me what my mind refuses? If this is hysteria, if it's psychological, then I can get better. I carry on practising the Lightening Process, but my symptoms persist.

One of the things that inevitably happens with long-term ME/CFS patients is that medical neglect inevitably occurs. This is partly because the sufferer feels so ill all the time and is so worn down and humiliated by repeated visits to doctors who tell them there is nothing wrong, so that they stop visiting GPs. In my case, because of my lowered immunity, I showed only slight signs of fever with respiratory infections. It's eight years later and I have a small bout of viral flu and have developed a slight cough. My GP tells me it's probably a viral chest infection, no treatment. Six months later my cough is still present. A chest X-ray detects double pneumonia in both lungs, but as I don't feel much different, the doctor gives me a seven-day course of amoxicillin, and tells me that will clear it up. Three months later a chest X-ray confirms the pneumonia is still there and the radiographer demands the GP order a CT scan. The scan comes back: I have collapsed lungs, moderate to severe bronchiectasis. I've been suffering from walking pneumonia for over 6 months. During that period, I've actually moved into a new house and carried on with everyday life as much as I can. As I feel ill all of the time, having pneumonia feels no different from having my normal ME/CFS symptoms.

I go and see a private specialist at the Brompton Hospital. He is also a specialist in weak immune systems. After many scans, he tells me I am very sick with damaged lungs, and he doesn't understand as my lungs were fine eight years before when I was being tested at Kings College hospital. I have a bronchoscopy and get immediately sick with sepsis and am rushed back into hospital. Over months and many hospital visits and lots of IV antibiotics, I am told I have atypical mycobacterium TB. It's the non-infectious kind that only people from developing countries or people who have very weak immune systems seem to come down with. Having sick lungs is frightening, and my lungs hurt and make me breathless on a regular basis, but it's not anywhere near as bad as having serious ME/CFS. I think the IV antibiotics have helped some of my ME symptoms; I seem to be able to do more walking and can go back to part-time psychoanalytic work. My Brompton consultant thinks my TB and ME are separate things, but one has led to the other. He says I probably had the ME/CFS first. I know my damaged lungs put my life at risk, but the joy of not being quite so ill with the fatigue comes rushing in. I'm not suffering so much pain, my colitis is not every single day, I can go for short walks, even swim gently in the sea. I have to be careful though. The addiction to life that makes up the life of every ME/CFS patient is that if they have a 'good day' – go for a short walk say, or a social event they enjoy – then the challenge is to not overdo it. But how do you stop yourself from overdoing living? How can you resist the energy flowing back into your limbs, the morning that comes and the headache that departs? How can stop running out to meet that day, with every bit of life you possess. In ME/CFS it's called boom and bust, the trick is even on a good day, you do nothing to conserve and build up your stores of energy. I have to confess I'm very bad at pacing, as it's called. I go swimming in the sea or take trips to London to visit friends and art galleries. I know perfectly well that doing these things, going out for dinner with my daughter, or making love to my partner, will put me in bed for days. But enjoyment, my pleasure principle, comes first and just over-rules everything else. Maybe that what's it's like to be an alcoholic, although I can't believe drinking is the same, it's never worth the inevitable hangover. The moment I feel even slightly better I feel like I'm on drugs, I want more and more of it. And then you are back in bed being very sick because you have pushed outside your allotted envelope of energy. And yet that pane of glass, smudged for so long, has started to show pink hues. I no longer feel like a creature bowed by my body, peering out. I can't live my life as I want to a lot of the time, but on some days, I do exactly that. With this illness living always costs such a lot, but the bursting exuberance when you come back into the world, albeit for such limited time, is a sheer delight, like no other I have experienced.

I'm having couple therapy with my partner, ostensibly about some wider conflicts and relationships in our family. The therapist is very good and specialises in working with couples where one person has been chronically ill. My partner incidentally has been a wonderful carer to me in my illness, he is an exquisite cook, who adapts to my many diets, and extremely kind, I know I would not have the semblance of health back that I have without his care. I also know not everyone is lucky enough to have a caring partner who stays the course; indeed, most relationships break up over long-term ME illness. Virginia Woolf has her nurse and carer in Leonard Woolf, and I've often thought and wondered whether she would have died earlier without his loving and tender presence. My illness doesn't really feature as part of the therapy until one day the therapist remarks on my illness. Its clear what she says she means as a compliment: 'You don't strike me as an ME patient.'

'Why not?'

'You are not all victimy in the way ME patients are.'

Silence. And then I reply, 'I'm just the opposite', and leave it at that. I want the therapy more than I want to challenge her on her prejudice, and afterwards I feel shame for not confronting her more explicitly. I'm so used to these views, and it's so exhausting having to combat them so consistently. It's like the response I get when I talk to hospital doctors or GPs, there is a familiar blank look that crosses their face when you start talking, like a shutter going down.

Because nobody knows ...

One day I hope with all my heart that there will be a cure for this illness, just as there has been for AIDS, or at least drugs that can alleviate the symptoms. As COVID-19 long-haul symptoms start to raise their heads with what is just another form of severe post-viral illness, maybe the world will finally wake up and become interested in ME/CFS. For this is the silent pandemic that has been carrying on for years and years, maybe even centuries (if we remember Alice James) under everybody's noses, before the pandemic we call COVID. Maybe, finally now this country will start funding research and stop listening to quacks like Simon Wessely, hailed from an age-old century, who have successfully psychosomatised one of the most severe and complex illnesses of the current age. Doctors are now less likely to believe COVID post-viral fatigue is imaginary as so many of them have actually caught it.

Over the years I have learnt slowly through the help of the doctors that do know something about ME/CFS how to combat the symptoms. Nick Panay is an excellent hormone specialist whose research focuses on the intersection of ME and hormone imbalance. Sarah Myhill, a GP specialising in ME, has been a controversial figure because she has turned to ecological methods or naturopathy to heal the immune system. In return, the medical community have repeatedly tried to strike her off the register. Sarah is maybe a maverick. I certainly don't agree with her views on vaccination, but I often wonder whether I would have simply ended up like Gregor, an insect stuck in bed, without her care. Through her, I learnt to consume a high-protein, no-sugar, paleo diet. My gut issues have been perhaps the hardest thing to address, because however many prebiotics and probiotics I consume the systemic candida I suffer has been hard to get treatment for, as intestinal candida in women is another thing most doctors don't believe in or treat. I take about 60 supplements a day and am continually revising what they are and if they work. It's super-expensive and time-consuming, but I know without my diet or my vitamins I would not have the limited health I now possess. Through my own research into the work of Dr Lerner and under Sarah's guidance, I have taken high doses of the anti-viral valacyclovir for 18 months. I don't know if they actually helped as I threw the kitchen sink at my illness, but what are people who are that ill supposed to do in the face of no treatment or the bonkers prescriptions from the PACE trial?

Although we live in a country with an NHS which, however depleted, is still meant to be free at the point of care, there is actually no NHS for ME/CFS patients, no treatments available whatsoever except the psychological treatments that become a smokescreen hiding the original picture. As Susan Sontag illustrated so beautifully in her book *Aids and its Metaphors*, illness is not just terrifying because it might cause death but because it dehumanises you: 'The most terrifying illnesses are those perceived not just as lethal but as dehumanising. Literally so' (Sontag, 2002 p. 38). Cancer and AIDS at the time Sontag was writing did not just kill, they disfigured. Cancer still does, and even if we can be killed by a heart attack or a massive stroke, the loss of breasts, hair or our wombs occurring in cancer marks it out as something that deforms us aesthetically and sexually. Sontag describes how cholera struck more fear than smallpox, because of the 'suddenness with which it struck and the indignity of the symptoms: fulminate diarrhoea and vomiting, whose result anticipated the horror of post-mortem decomposition' (Sontag, 2002, p. 39). My symptoms of ME/CFS have not been unlike cholera symptoms, albeit more intermittent. But the point Sontag is making is that illness carries different levels of shame and stigma. The more shameful the illness, the more secret it becomes, with AIDS there was and is impugned guilt, the infection through sex, and the communities designated as contaminating. Diseases like AIDS, leprosy, syphilis and cholera are the ones that seem particularly susceptible to promotion to 'plague'.

TB has always had a more romantic association, a slower demise, as depicted by Milly Theale in Henry James's *Wings of a Dove*. Terminally ill, but beautiful and ethereal, rather than ravished and repulsive, Milly Theale is the moral compass for the other characters in the novel. And yet Milly (who is based on Henry James's beloved cousin, Minnie Temple, who died young) is rather more than just being a martyr's grave, into which much literary criticism has thrown her. On the contrary Milly is someone who tries to get up every morning, who strives to choose to live every day. As her physician Sir Luke Strett advised her, 'isn't to "live" exactly what I'm trying to persuade you to take the trouble to do?' (James, 2003, p. 213). Rather than being alienating or a contaminating menace, Milly is seen as someone who inspires, and even morally transforms the other characters like Densher, who grows to love her. The most interesting part about Milly is arguably not her moral influence over others, but the flame of her own desire, which is tragically extinguished when she learns of the plot between Densher and Kate to steal her fortune. And yet for all her strength and weakness, Milly remains enigmatic, an elusive presence which is presaged on the reader being given absolutely no physical details about her disease. With my own non-infectious TB or mycobacterium there is no treatment as my immune system is apparently too weak to cope with the vicious drug regime necessary to break the thick outer walls of these fungal pathogens. Mycobacterium is opportunistic in the sense that many people carry the organisms, which are found in water and soil; but it is only when your immune system is very weak that this fungal bacillus can actually invade the lungs. It's a silent illness, and like ME/CFS something that doctors know currently very little about. But the ignominy attached to my TB is negligible and non-existent compared to the mortification of having ME, because like Alice James's 'lump of granite' in the breast, my TB is there as a pocket and scar on my lungs, for every doctor to see. There is no blank face in response to this illness, there is dignity and sympathy conferred, whereas with ME the loss of face is not just the real hell of your symptoms, but the knowledge that you are being seen as someone who is quixotic, whose disease is entirely chimerical and neurotic.

It's March 2020, and COVID-19 is hitting. We watch the pandemic move out of Wuhan and China, and slowly roll towards Europe. News footage of hospitals, corpses and desperation as death marches inexorably through Italy. We listen and watch; it's ominous and yet unreal. Nevertheless, I spend a day at my daughter's house watching a therapy

talk online as we are being too cautious to travel to London to participate in person. Within the next couple of days my daughter comes down
with what everyone thinks is probably COVID: intense flu, with a
hacking cough. Five days later I come down with it too. Normally my
symptoms with any infection are mild, but I have feverish chills that
speed from 39°C to 35°C, and then back up again. One minute I'm
burning and the next I'm shivering, shaking in my bed – cold as ice. It's
night-time, and I recognise the symptoms of pneumonia, so I dial 111.
The paramedic triages me, and then nothing, until a doctor rings me in
the morning. She talks in a flat exhausted voice, 'don't come into hospital unless you feel near death, you are safer at home'. I ring my GP, who
gamely says he will don a hazmat suit and come and examine me. But
then my respiratory team ring and tell me to come into hospital unac-
companied. I'm being admitted to the COVID ward. My husband cries,
he doesn't want me to go, and the really nice GP from my surgery has to
persuade him it's for the best. We drive eerily through a deserted
Brighton to the hospital, and hug each other, we are both in tears. I get
out of the car and walk through the doors of A&E.

It feels like the most surreal day of my life. I am shown to the COVID
ward (actually it's a bay) just round the back of the emergency unit. No
one seems to be wearing enough PPE, the elderly patients that are mobile
don't bother with masks and the nursing staff just have paper ones and
flimsy aprons. The other patients are all in bed gasping into oxygen
masks. I'm scared, but then again being scared is nothing new. I'm more
than slightly out of it; they swab me, take bloods and chest X-rays.
Luckily, it's only a normal pneumonia, so I'm not heading for intensive
care and my imagined, impersonal death attached to a ventilator.
Instead, I'm given lots of antibiotics and after a couple of days sent
home. As I leave the ward, the televisions are flickering, and Boris
Johnson is announcing lockdown.

Viruses are much more frightening and primitive than bacteria. Many
new degenerative autoimmune diseases of the nervous system and brain
such as multiple sclerosis are now being seen as being caused by slow-
acting viruses, unlike ME, which is still resolutely bracketed as psychological. As Sontag writes, 'Viruses are not simply agents of infection,
contamination. They transport genetic "information", they transform
cells.' Viruses evolve and mutate and insidiously stalk us. No wonder
COVID-19 gets framed as a conspiracy – a plague that is everywhere and
seemingly nowhere. COVID-19 has taken the world by a quiet storm,
one that feels more like a slow inexorable creep. And like AIDS, it's a
virus that can invade and advance with rapidity to literally eat up the
lungs, or it can linger in a more slow-acting way and then strike with

blood clots in any of the major organs. I'm at a post-COVID review at the hospital, because of long haul COVID symptoms, which for me present as just more inflammation and breathlessness in my lungs which is not signalling infection. The respiratory registrar 'Tom' asks me a series of questions about the nature of my COVID illness and runs numerous tests and scans. After they are finished, he calls me aside for a chat.

'Luckily you don't have any lung or heart clots and there is nothing new on your chest X-ray.'

'But what about my ongoing chest pain? That's not my lung disease.'

'That's just more inflammation, there is no treatment at the moment, it's just another form of post-viral fatigue.'

'Not so different from my ME then?'

He looks at me thoughtfully. 'I think that's going to be the conclusion we all eventually come to. Inflammation of all systems in the body. But at the moment nobody really knows ...'

So, at last we are beginning to see a decisive shift in how doctors are being able to observe and listen to symptoms of ME and acknowledge their veracity. In July 2020, CNN news reported on remarks made by Dr Anthony Fauci, President Trump's top medical advisor, on the similarities between COVID-19 long-haul symptoms and ME/CFS:

> There may well be a post-viral syndrome associated with COVID-19 ... If you look anecdotally, there is no question that there are a number of individuals who have a post-viral syndrome that in many respects incapacitates them for weeks and weeks following so called recovery ... There are chat rooms you click on and see people who recovered that really do not get back to normal. They report symptoms such as brain fog, difficulty concentrating and fatigue that resemble the symptoms of ME.

Anne Boyer doesn't really agree with Elaine Scarry's idea that pain destroys language. She argues:

> Pain doesn't destroy language: it changes it. What is difficult is not impossible ... pain is widely declared inarticulate for the reason we are not supposed to share a language for how we really feel ...
>
> (Boyer, 2019, p. 213)

Boyer believes that the silence of pain is a lie; pain inflicts an over communicability, a drive to take away the pain of another, provoking 'an impossible-to-bear sympathetic discomfort – sometimes in the form of annoyance, sometimes in the form of anxiety, sometimes in the form of pity – upon oneself'. Pain in other words doesn't just make the subject furious and frightened, it makes everyone else feel those things too. Think of the power and sheer unendurability of a baby screaming. When the witness can't see what's causing the anguish, and feels powerless to alleviate what is sensed to be violent and threatening, then an answering violence comes in the form of disavowal and denial. Just imagine we didn't believe in the phenomenon of depression or trauma, or that painful experiences such as loss and bereavement needed to be talked about and shared. Imagine what it would be like to lose someone you loved, and everyone refused to believe you? Pain and illness do not literally destroy language, but that language is rendered completely ineffective, null and void, if other people can't speak or listen to it. In psychoanalysis, people who can't bear what they feel, and whose feelings are more often than not too much for everybody else, are diagnosed with having borderline personality. As if it's possible to have a personality disorder. None of us can bear everything we feel, which is why repression is historically so necessary. Children repress, what's beyond their ability to either process or experience. And with physical illness we are all on the borderline, personally speaking of what we can experience, process and share. In psychoanalysis we listen not just to the language spoken (or the signifier as Lacan would say), but to all the signifying silences of feelings, symptoms and half articulated experiences that exist in the spaces in-between language and speech. You learn if you are to be good at what you do, to listen to the gaps, the clearances in between the wood of words, as well as to the language spoken. And most of all you listen carefully to the symptoms and to the unbearable things unspoken. One of the necessary repressions perhaps with this illness is the economical way many sufferers will minimise their illness, not just because it's not listened to properly but because chronic illness and pain over time becomes boring, and all consuming. The trick is how to live your life around your symptoms, without becoming an invalid. Alice James, who arguably suffered from ME for most of her adult life, became very angry on reading George Eliot's letters, exclaiming, 'What an abject coward she seems to have been about physical pain, as if it weren't degrading enough to have headaches, without jotting them down to stare at for all time' (James, 1987, p. 41).

Alice was acutely aware of how she was perceived as sick and hysterical, and confined to a kind of hyper-feminine role. Thus, she did not want her own writing to be seen 'as a vehicle for a moan', a fate George Eliot was spared 'given her public writing career' (James, 1987, p. 124). This an acute issue for the patients who have ME, even those well enough to put pen to paper. Being a psychoanalyst has helped me in a myriad of ways, despite my occasional wobbles, in being able to see through the hysteria literature, both within my profession and outside of it. I also have quite a few clients with this condition, more since the advent of COVID-19, and it's enabling to be able to listen to their symptoms, both physical and psychological and know I am equipped to really listen to them.

Psychoanalysis has had an important role in the psychosomatic framing of physical disease into mental illness. Many of the early followers of Freud, saw mental illness in a Nietzschean way as a failure of the will. Alfred Adler saw psychoanalysis as primarily about the individual's need for superiority, their will to power. And of course, physical illness is then deemed a symptom of being weak or sick mentally. When Freud became ill with cancer, his friend Ferenczi offered to analyse him. Whereas, Wilhelm Reich, saw his illness as evidence of his misery and repressed genital sexuality. Cancer was, for Reich, a deadly orgone energy that results from a repressed sexual life and literally not enough orgasms. Reich's view of Freud's cancer, which led onto his belief of any cancer, was that it was evidence of resignation, a giving up of hope: 'If my view of cancer is correct, you just give up, you resign, and then you shrink' (Reich, 1975, p. 33).

For Reich, Freud was unhappy because of his normative bourgeois marriage and his lack of sex. He writes:

> But there is little doubt that he was very much dissatisfied genitally. Both his resignation and his cancer were evidence of that. Freud had to give up as a person, had to give up personal pleasures, personal delights in his middle years ... he, himself, had to give up.
>
> (Reich, 1975, p. 33)

Freud, especially in the way he dealt with his cancer, was a walking example of not giving up in a good way. He never allowed himself to be invalided. Whilst he didn't believe in happiness as a permanent state, his personal and family life seemed very happy. He was passionate enough with Martha before their marriage, and then came six children. Freud was always dedicated to his work in creating psychoanalysis, and on providing for his family. If his sex drive, in middle age, faltered because Martha wanted no more children, maybe his understanding of her has been overlooked. If Freud didn't eventually practice the sex he preached, he had plenty to sublimate it with. He was a loving man, very different from Reich's furious and unstable character. His containment and politeness didn't mean he was repressed. In fact, Freud's desire in relation to women and men never seemed to desert him. We can see Reich's comments on Freud's cancer, caricaturing him as a shrinking man, as both cruel and envious. Although Reich really did believe cancer was negative orgone energy, he even wrote a book about it called *The Cancer Biopathy*. Reich's ideas about the mind and body were in his early years left wing, but there was always a simplicity to his thinking. His idea, for example, that capitalism was the death-drive infuriated Freud, much like the orgone theory, everything becomes reducible to either an external force, or a literal and translatable body. If Freud believed hope lived in the id, it was because he perceived, like his favourite pupil Ferenczi, that it was the affective telepathic force or communication within the transference, that moves or promotes change. Not some simple body release or 'streaming' that Reich spoke of.

The truth is the affectual body is secretive, it might speak incessantly at times but that doesn't mean we have the language or the mind, for that matter, to mediate or make sense of it. The unconscious, our affectual life, is unknowable, until it is brought into a mistake ridden perception. The body is observable, but what we see is not always the truth. As Michel Henry has so comprehensively shown there is an inner manifestation of the body, a life-force, that can't be seen, or captured in the literal way Reich spoke about sexual release. What Freud understood and, in a sense lived, was that the body as a life-force is vastly more complex than simply an evacuation of what we feel. This life-force, our pleasure principle, is something we can enjoy but often it's also what we must bear and endure. On his 79th birthday Freud has 'violent pain' trying to insert his prosthesis, he is recovering from yet another operation. So, another version of the 'monster' must be started that day by Pichler. His doctor Schur describes the crisis and its aftermath: 'This is one of the very few occasions on which Freud felt somewhat desperate. Yet he soon regained control and in Pichler's office was again his composed, patient and polite self' (Freud, 1992, p. 185).

A few days later, Freud writes in his diary:

> Hesitantly a beautiful spring is unfolding before our eyes this year and I would not have too much to complain about if fate had not sent me a birthday present for May 6, the necessity of having the prosthesis remade, which naturally involved an extraordinary amount of torture.
>
> (Freud, 1992, p. 185)

Freud's suffering from his monstrous illness gives way to a form of hope we can only call transience, his words, here, so reminiscent of his well-known paper. The relief and hope that comes with the lessening of his symptoms, in the full knowledge that the winter of his pain will return, again. Reich's orgone theory sparked the 1960s wave of body therapies, that continues to this day. But however soothing body therapy might be, and I have tried many different kinds to alleviate the symptoms of my ME. It can't cure us of the life force, that is both the pleasure of our body and its curse: the illness and death that eventually presents itself. This life force is unconscious and remains mysterious until it surfaces, and so how we read the body matters. The point is that the body remains a mystery. Illness like trauma, might be the score that the body keeps, but it's also a secret tally; there is only so much we can ever really know. TB until the advent of antibiotics was one of the most romanticised and terrible diseases of its day. Today, given that antibiotics are resistant to my type of TB, nobody knows what the progress is quite going to be.

I've sought out and found many amazing doctors in my years of being ill, especially the consultants at Kings and my current lung specialists at the Brompton and in Brighton. And yet none of them have been able to help me with my ME/CFS. I once talked to another Registrar at the Sussex County Hospital in Brighton in the middle of the initial bouts of pneumonia. He was different and seemed interested in my ME in a way no other doctor really has been, and he kept asking me about Sarah Myhill's work. And then suddenly it was as if our roles were reversed, and he started talking to me conspiratorially as though it was some kind of secret conversation:

> I have this friend, and his wife has ME, she is pregnant and bed-bound, and because we are all taught in medical school it's a psychiatric disorder he doesn't know what to do. Would your doctor Sarah Myhill help? My friend is going to have to give up his career to look after his partner when the baby comes and then there will be no salary. He is pretty desperate ...

I replied:

> Sarah's waiting list has been closed for years but her website is very good, and you can ask me anything you want. I know about some of the available protocols, its mostly vitamins, pacing and diet.

We talked for a while and then before I left, he said, 'Please don't tell anyone we had this conversation, I'd be sacked.' I just said 'of course', but it was only as I was leaving the hospital, I realised that the doctor he was referring to was actually himself ...

With ME/CFS it's a secret, because no one is fully believed and no one really knows how to name or treat the condition, then it becomes easy to stop listening to the pain of the patient. Illness is not just an individual body, it's a collective one, and without the right kind of listening how can these patients find their experience comprehensible? Or how can it be shared and made sense of by others? It's like navigating black holes, or outer space. With the advent of COVID-19 we are going to see much more post-viral fatigue illness, and we need more than ever to publicly acknowledge the nature and the history of ME/CFS. We need to address the collective disavowal of this illness that has made certain psychiatrists and psychologists rich and famous, but has condemned thousands of sufferers to their lonely and private agony. In re-addressing the whole sham narrative of ME as women's hysteria, we need to address the cultural amnesia and shame that silences these victims and so hasten future medical research that might bring about a cure. If Freud was alive today, he would be horrified.

To the ME/CFS community, I send all my hope and love, even if that hope, at the present time, is simply for a transience of the symptoms.

References

Appignanesi, L. and Forrester, J. (2005) *Freud's Women*, London, Phoenix.

Boyer, A. (2019) *The Undying: A Meditation on Modern Illness*, London, Penguin Books.

Freud, S. (1992) *The Diary of Sigmund Freud, 1929–1939: A Record of The Final Decade*, translated, annotated and with an introduction by M. Molnar, New York, Scribner.

Hooper, M. (2012) Prof Wessely's Award of the Inaugural John Maddox Prize for his Courage in the Field of ME and Gulf War Syndrome, 12 November, retrieved from www.margaretwilliams.me/2012/wessely-maddox-prize_12nov2012.pdf.

James, A. (1987) *The Diary of Alice James*, Harmondsworth, Penguin.

James, H. (2003) *The Wings of a Dove*, London, Penguin.

Kafka, F. (1988) The Metamorphosis, in *The Collected short Stories of Franz Kafka*, pp. 89–140, London, Penguin Books.

Kafka, F. (2016) *Letters to Friends, Family and Editions*, translated by R. Winston and C. Winston, New York, Schoken Books.

Klimas, N. (2015) Dr. Nancy Klimas, retrieved from www.healthrising.org/chronic-fatigue-syndrome-mecfs-doctor-resource-center/dr-nancy-klimas-chronic-fatigue-syndrome-treatmentinstitute-for-neuroimmune-research-nova-southeastern-ft-lauderdale-fl.

Lazaridis, N (2003) Sigmund's Freud's Oral Cancer, *British Journal of Maxillofacial Surgery*, 41, pp. 78–83.

Reich W. (1975) *Reich Speaks of Freud*, Harmondsworth, Pelican.

Shepherd, C. (2015) It's Time for Doctors to Apologise to Their ME Patients, *The Telegraph*, 7 December, retrieved from www.telegraph.co.uk/news/health/ 12033810/Its-time-for-doctors-to-apologise-to-their-ME-patients.html.

Scarry, E. (1987) *The Body in Pain: The Making and Unmaking of the World*, Oxford, Oxford University Press.

Sedgwick, E. K. (2006) *A Dialogue On Love*, Boston, MA, Beacon Press.

Sontag S. (2002) *Illness as a Metaphor & Aids and its Metaphors*, London, Penguin Books.

Showalter, E. (1998) *Hystories: Hysterical Epidemics and Modern Culture*, London, Picador.

Wessely, S. (1990) Chronic Fatigue and Myalgia Syndromes, in *Psychological Disorders in General Medical Settings*, pp. 82–98, Lewiston, NY, Hogrefe & Huber.

Wessely, S., David, A., Butler, S. and Chalder, T. (1989) Management of the Chronic (Postviral) Fatigue Syndrome, *Journal of The Royal College of General Practitioners*, 39, pp. 26–29.

Wessely, S., Hotopf, M. and Sharpe, M. (1998) *Chronic Fatigue and its Syndromes*, Oxford, Oxford University Press.

Woolf, V. (2012) *On Being Ill*, Ashfield, MA, Paris Press.

6   Beyond Reparation

Part One

An evil man hides behind, or underneath, a child. To kill him you also
have to kill the child. So, you do, because your sense of righteousness
and reparation demands it. And, in murdering the child, innocently
protecting yourself and your fellow countrymen against your enemy, you
join this man in his atrocity. Hope is thus extinguished for everybody.
This is a description of the Israel and Gaza war, where thousands of
children have been massacred, exterminated on a daily basis in order to
protect a nation, a group, secure borders, a homeland ... There are sides,
and histories and intergenerational traumas where grief is unassuaged.
Populations who have been in turn displaced and annihilated in
unspeakable ways can lead to a demand for restoration. Violence is
always on the side of the reparation of my hurt, it's an entitlement
which attaches itself incessantly to my wounded past. The restitution of
what was taken. And as such it remains completely amnesic to other
stories and other humanities.

Hope based on reparation is a false ideal which will always return us
to the most furious grudge of what we have been deprived of; what has
been taken. In Kleinian psychoanalysis, reparation is part of her famous
notion of the depressive position where guilt over aggressive impulses
gives way to the ability to repair the damaged object. Reparation, here,
is to the other, where persecutory guilt gives way to penitence. Cycles of
virtue and reparation repair the cycles of violence and restore the good
objects we have killed or destroyed. But this need for repair is always a
return to the original pain or wound. And this makes reparation cir-
cular, how do we really move beyond the demand for reparation, whether this demand comes from the victim or the super-ego? What really is
the difference between the demand for reparation and the guilt that
meets it? In psychoanalysis, in therapy and in life, there is the need to

DOI: 10.4324/9781003515777-6

return to our childhoods and our past traumas so they can be healed and restored. But repair is an illusion. We can't repair our childhoods, our parents, or our past traumas, however strong the belief or hope. Reparation we could say is a Kleinian cause, but we should be wary of such hope, as it is arguably a defence against exploration of the complexity and not just of ourselves, but also other people.

Causes are often virtuous, and very often, as James Baldwin tells us, extremely bloodthirsty. In his analysis of Harriet Beecher Stowe's *Uncle Tom's Cabin*, Baldwin discusses how within the limitless descriptions of mindless brutality in the book, Stowe is moved to state that slavery is wrong and 'perfectly horrible', but nowhere does she explore or even ask why her people are motivated to diminish black people in this way (Baldwin, 1998, p. 12). Sentimentality, exemplified by the humble emasculated figure of Uncle Tom, envisages his salvation by his suffering. It is only through incessant mortification of his own flesh that Uncle Tom can be spiritually cleansed and whitened and so 'enter into communion with God or man'. Stowe's good work is, in Baldwin's view, her own fear of sinning, of being cast into the flames. It is her shameless bargain 'before the throne of grace; God and salvation becoming her personal property, purchased with the coin of her virtue' (Baldwin, 1998, p. 14).

It is our fear and dread of human beings that terrorises us and fuels our racism; our need in Baldwin's words to cut a human being 'down to size'. Truth then resides in exploring the mixture of 'ambiguity, paradox, this hunger, danger and darkness' that resides in all of us (Baldwin, 1998, p. 13). We are always more, more unknowable or unpredictable than we think, and of course the same applies to other people. In evading the other person's complexity, 'which is nothing more than the disquieting complexity of ourselves – we are diminished ...' (Baldwin, 1998, p. 13).

The circles of reparation that return us to trauma, risk a virtuous denial of the complexity, the unknowability of ourselves and of course other people. We can't know the unconscious, until it becomes part of our ego, our consciousness. And so, our unconsciousness, and other people's, is a potential for better or worse, but it can't be known as such until it enters our experience. Therapists risk this evasion of complexity when they start categorising the unconscious as anything certain, as though it can simply be fished out of a session by the right interpretation or realised by the right chain of linguistic signification. Both interpretation and free association are perhaps the two most established forms of bringing unconscious material into the light, but they are no more than a form of imaginative guesswork. These techniques aren't truths, however much they might be helpful in analytic work. The evidence, or proof of these techniques lies in the becoming, the experience that unfolds. As

William James might say, it's the praxis of life spreading between the two people in an analytic session that enables us to understand what has provoked it. And yet, as none of us are just one, but many, the complexity of who we are and whom we are facing is far more difficult an encounter that any single 'truth' or understanding, can provide. So, any psychoanalytic theory that claims a too knowing ideology of the unconscious runs the risk of simplification. Whatever the merits of a Kleinian and Lacanian approach, and there are many interesting features of both theories; they, remain simplified if they over-promise or clarify a particular method. None of us can be over-confident as to what our unconscious contains. After all, it is only understood, once it has ceased to exist; when it moves through ego formations into what is communicable and realisable. And so, the unconscious can't be explained as solely following linguistic signifiers, or as holding persecutory fantasies. It is much more mysterious than the logic of a particular system. One reason, perhaps, why hope for psychoanalysis, can't reside as a faith in any of its founding fathers or mothers. Like any child such hope must venture forth and explore a world of affinity and difference. Trainings in psychoanalysis would benefit from more curiosity about what literatures and cultural texts offer students who are starting out. Just learning Klein, or Lacan, or Freud for that matter, won't serve analysis by getting us anywhere new. It will just be like an Oedipus, or a Hamlet, repeating a too familiar story, identifying with, or mimicking, Mum and Dad, without any real adventure into the new potential of whom we can become.

Kleinian theory at its most pure, gives a rather unrealistic hope, or despair, about the unconscious and what it consists of, and not enough credence to the importance of the ego. Klein and her followers believed that a determined analysis of the child's deepest psychotic fantasies would produce relief and release from such aggression. In Klein's most infamous and dogged pursuit of these anxieties, in *Narrative of a Child Analysis*, she analyses a ten-year-old child, 'Richard'. In this therapy she continuously describes the child's frightening inner world of persecutory objects to him (Klein, 1998, p. 99). Whether these interpretations are the truth of Richard's unconscious we don't know, none of us can actually know anybody's unconscious material. Nevertheless, Klein is sure. After a particularly terrifying series of observations where Klein remarks on how Richard has devoured everybody, he picks up a figure in a red coat symbolising Klein and bites it. Klein responds with assuring him that she has been 'included in the disaster' (Klein, 1998, p. 99). Richard gets worried and starts wondering what Klein will be doing in the afternoon, whereupon Klein tells him he needs proof that he hasn't completely killed off both her and his mummy. Richard's response is to leave his toys and jump manically around trying to get Klein to enjoy with him the view out of the window, onto the countryside. And Klein feels satisfied that he has been substantially relieved of his fears and able to focus more on the external world.

This is what Klein actually says about the work:

> This is an instance of the relief obtained from the interpretation of very frightening and painful material ... It is in fact striking that very painful interpretations referring to death and to dead internalised objects, which is psychotic anxiety – could have the effect of reviving hope and making the patient feel more alive. My explanation for this would be that bringing a very deep anxiety nearer to consciousness, in itself produces relief. But I also believe that the very fact that the analysis gets into contact with deep-lying unconscious anxieties gives the patient a feeling of being understood and therefore revives hope.
>
> (Klein, 1998, pp. 99–100)

We can only contrast this invasive technique with Anna Freud's more gentle approach, which did not believe in analysing children in such adult transference terms. Anna Freud clearly believed children couldn't cope with such ruthless deconstructions of their minds, putting forward a technique that strengthened an alliance with the therapist as a good object (Freud, 1971). Melanie Klein's and Anna Freud's different approaches, drawn up in the oppositional 'controversial discussions', have historically polarised an emphasis on the unconscious (Klein) and ego defences (Anna Freud). So much so that Klein has been heralded as the true inheritor of Freud's ideas, rather than his daughter.

There can be no truth to the unconscious in terms of knowing what it is. And ego defences are not just troublesome things we have to get out the way, they are essential. Not just in protecting us from the traumas of our past; they are also the forms that once they can move, can more flexibly enable our freedom and our future. The ego, as I have argued elsewhere, is something that is, in part, telepathically created between the mother and child. And although it has a seat in unconscious fantasy, it is not purely the unified or completely imaginary entity that Lacan envisages. The ego is made up of differing forms that can either limit or expand our experience. The more plural the forms, the more flexible the ego becomes, and the more able it is in moving our unconscious into our thought and felt life. Trauma is often a repression or a dissociation of what we cannot fully experience or are unable to remember. Because it exceeds our ability to bear or process what we have undergone; it can arguably be re-membered within therapy through the creation of new ego forms. But how we remember, what re-memory really is, and what the unconscious contributes to memory remains an open and interesting question. We are not just one thing. There is an intrinsic idea in Kleinian thinking that once you confront the horror of your most persecutory unconscious anxiety, it is a kind of truth that will free you. And I disagree. I don't think having your inner persecution confronted in the stark way that Klein describes would ever work with an adult so why would it work with a child? When someone comes into therapy with a history of severe childhood trauma, the last thing you do is to start interpreting it, without any preamble. You don't set out to find it, you wait for it to emerge. Trauma is, by definition, not something that happens to us, it happens to someone else, the part of ourselves we can't bear witness to. You are absent on some level from the event because it's simply too raw or unbearable to process. In Bion's terminology, trauma is an excess of raw beta elements which the alpha functioning of the mind can't contain or digest. You can't simply release trauma from the body or the mind, because you have never fully experienced it. With trauma you work with the early defences to move them so they can serve the present person in a more enlarging or a more enlivening way. Working with ego defences allows them to move and to hopefully bend and expand, to embody more extensively our experience.

When the trauma is very terrible maybe therapeutic work is not to investigate, or to invade, for that always risks a return to a place that is unbearable. We are never just one identity, one history, one trauma. We are multiple beings, with differing histories, separate stories, past and present, that go to make up who we are. Confronting Hamas or the Israeli government with the horror of their murder or genocide isn't going to be successful. They will only feel their own wound, not the horror they inflict on others in the name of its necessary reparation. My fantasy of Richard biting the little figure in the red coat, which is Klein, becomes his fury with her for turning him into a beta-wolf. Followed by his need to jolly her away from what he can't take anymore by a precocious ego defence to get her more interested in the weather or the pretty scenery.

At the end of *Culture and Imperialism*, the late Edward Said makes this simple but very profound statement:

> No one today is purely *one* thing. Labels like Indian, or woman, or Muslim, or American are no more than starting points, which if followed into actual experience for only a moment are quickly left

behind. Imperialism consolidated the mixture of cultures and identities on a global scale. But its worst and most paradoxical gift was to allow people to believe that they were only, mainly, exclusively, white, or black, or Western, or Oriental. Yet just as human beings make their own history, they make their cultural and ethnic identities. No one can deny the persisting continuities of long traditions, sustained habitations, national languages, and cultural geographies, but there seems no reason except fear and prejudice to keep insisting on their separation and distinctiveness, as if that was all human life was about.

(Said, 1994, pp. 407–408)

No one in psychoanalysis is just one thing. Richard's wolf aggression, and Klein's, sometimes it is hard to distinguish one from the other, is the animal Klein hunts. In successfully interpreting the aggressive fantasies she aims to alleviate Richard's anxiety. And in her account of the analysis, it is a success. Richard's persecutory and idealised fantasies are worked through to a point where he can acknowledge and love his mother as a whole object, garner relief from his persecutory anxieties about his father and feel the necessary hope and reparation in relation to the depressive position.

Richard's analysis was in the middle of World War Two, and much of Richard's mind was focused on the invasion of Germany across Europe. Hitler being the enemy or persecutory penis identification in Klein's thinking, against which Richard and the good allies fought back to conquer as many countries or mother lands as possible. It is perhaps not incidental that Richard's older brother was in the British army at the time of his analysis, and his own house had been bombed. Klein herself had taken refuge from the bombs in Scotland when she was writing up her notes. So, both Richard and Klein were arguably to some extent suffering from war trauma. Klein, however, is clearly interested in the internal war going on in Richard not the very obvious and external one going on all around them. Richard's anxieties are thus all located within internal Oedipal conflicts. Reparation finally arrives, along with hope:

[Richard] becomes capable of feeling sympathy for the destroyed enemy. This was shown, for instance, when he became identified with the sunk *Prinz Eugen* … This hopefulness, and his ability to maintain a good relation to the analyst as an internal and external object, in spite of resentment, feeling of loss, and great anxiety, confirm my view that as a result of his analysis the good internal object was much more firmly established in Richard.

(Klein, 1998, p. 466)

Mitigation of Richard's hate with love is evidenced by the reparative hope he displays towards Klein and the German enemy in his last few sessions. But how do we know if Richard's more needy behaviour at the end of his therapy, towards Klein, is really the resolution of his internal world she seems to think. Or whether it is more a case of what Anna Freud would call a 'treatment compliance'. Interpretation of the child's fantasies and transference were the alpha and omega of analysis according to Klein. But if we think of this with respect to adult therapy such an approach simply misses all the other things going on within the therapy, unconscious perception, unconscious communication, unconscious transference not exclusively onto the therapist but can be in a Freudian sense onto any object. And who is the interpretation for? Is it for the benefit of the patient or the analyst? The difficulty of the persistent and heavy interpretation Klein advocated, based on her own particular internal world view, is that it brooked no arguments. The danger for the therapy is that such interpretation produces sadomasochism and infantilises the patient, quite apart from the scene of trauma which it too easily reproduces. Questioning becomes resistance and yielding the only hopeful result. It's an approach that can sound like the language of war, or an invasion, with absolutely no doubt about the winning side.

The 24th session between Klein and Richard begins. He is slightly late and appears frightened and unhappy. Klein links his wish to run away with his resistance the day before:

> In the previous session she had interpreted to him his doubts of Mummy and herself (the wicked brute). Yesterday on leaving the playroom, he had said that on the previous day she had left the window open and it should have been shut. This remark also expressed his grievance against the wicked brute-mother and Mrs K. They should not have left the window – standing for the genital – open, which allowed the brute octopus, the bad father, to have sexual intercourse and to get inside.
>
> (Klein, 1998, p. 111)

Richard replies that 'he could not possibly wish to attack and abuse Mrs K. and Mummy; it made him unhappy even to think he could wish to do that'. Richard goes back to drawings of the war, colouring countries he is invading red, and countries he has conquered light blue reminding him of his mother. Meanwhile, the black centre of the map representing Daddy is 'squeezed in' and cornered. All a perfect geographical reproduction of the Oedipal conflicts, Klein is constantly reiterating. Outer space seemingly chimes harmoniously with internal space. Then Richard rebels with an astute question. He pauses, looks up at Klein and says, 'Do I really think this of all of you? I don't know if I do. How can you really know what I think?' (Klein, 1998, p. 111).

For Lacan, Klein's analysis works not because it reduces his anxiety but because it literally plasters the Oedipal complex onto Richard, providing a symbolic language and his access to it, in place of his imaginary realities. Where Lacan and Klein meet on the treatment of Richard is that they use the case history to prove their very different meta-psychologies. And it's the theory that wins out. The analyst's interpretations, their ideologies, if you like, take precedence over the more complex history or unconscious of either the child or the individual. It's not that the Oedipal complex does not exist within Richard, it is clearly present in his drawings, arrived at or created by Klein's interpretations. The question of the therapy might be, given the sadomasochism of Richard's external and internal war, what options would ameliorate that fight or trauma?

In the current war between Israel and Hamas, we have two opposing narratives of reparation and symbolic naming that are vying for the claim on a homeland. Jonathan Freedland, in a *Guardian* article, cautions us to know our enemy and our ally. He argues that calls for a ceasefire misunderstand the murderous nature of Hamas, who are not freedom fighters but 'violent jihadists'. He writes:

> 'Violent jihadism is not a rhetorical pose: it is Hamas's animating creed.' We mustn't make the liberal assumption that Hamas can listen to negotiations, they don't care how many of their children are slaughtered, their murderous intent to kill Jewish people in Israel is fundamental. And that is why the West is right to agree with Israel, that Hamas 'cannot be temporarily deterred', it must be defeated.
>
> (Freedland, 2023)

On the other side Freedland notes the right-wing extremity of the Israeli government, some of whom have terrorist histories of their own. Extremists that arm the illegal Israeli settlers of the West Bank and encourage the campaign of murder and violence against Palestinians. Freedland ends his piece by stating that:

> So Washington, Brussels and London currently back Israel because they agree that no peace is possible without the removal of Hamas. They are much less clear that no peace is possible without the removal of Netanyahu and his henchman. Yet both can be true.
>
> (Freedland, 2023)

And yet, thousands of people who live in the West, including Jewish people, don't support either Hamas or Netanyahu; they are equally horrified by the violence of Hamas and of Israel's government; they just want the killing to stop. Nuances of Freedland's arguments are not difficult to grasp, they are perfectly clear. These people, who want an end to the violence, want a ceasefire precisely because they can see that the aggression propagated by each group is totally blind to the suffering on the other side. Excuses for the violence of Hamas (as freedom fighters) or Israel (their right to a homeland that has arguably dispossessed another people) are causes that can be seen as noble, particularly to the clan or kinship group they belong to. But the restoration demanded is as brutal as it is blind. Reparation in relation to our childhood, our parents, even for a homeland that had been stolen or denied doesn't work.

Hope can't be based on the need for restitution of our past wounds or traumas, it has to be grounded in the grief and the loss of what we leave behind. Violence whatever else it is, is always a giving up in a bad way, a foreclosure of other paths and future possibilities. It is deaf and dumb and blind to anything but the delirium which drives it. As such it is an escape from pain and suffering and loss. Violence is what Robert Stoller would call the triumphant solution in a sadomasochist scenario. Where the victimised, bombed, mutilated child I remember being, and can't recover from, is evacuated and located in the enemy whom I have reduced to rubble. Only then I am free, only then am I able to bear the shame of my once victimised existence. Except this triumph is false and must be repeated, over and over again to succeed.

Harold Searles was a gifted psychoanalyst who probably worked with more psychotic patients than most. His work is humbling because of its emotionally integrity and perhaps because he, as a therapist, was apparently so loving. Although Searles is influenced by many of Klein's ideas, particularly the idea that we all have a psychotic primitive core, he mediates this with his approach to the transference. For Searles, therapy is a mutual enterprise with each participant contributing to the material. He never names the clinical work as unconscious telepathic communication. But it is arguable from the accounts of therapy he presents, that this is what he understands to be happening.

Searles understood the vengefulness that many of his 'borderline' patients presented with as being due to an inability to mourn and grieve. And this inability to bear loss was linked to past trauma, often intergenerational. In his paper 'The Psychodynamics of Vengefulness' (1956), Searles writes:

In my experience, patients do not become free from a crippling thirst for revenge merely by working through the hostility residing therein. Not until the therapy has gone onto achieve a working through of the deeper-lying grief and separation anxiety is the foundation for vengefulness eradicated.

(Searles, 1986, p. 177)

Grief and separation anxiety are of course not the same thing. Vengefulness, for Searles is a way of holding onto a person and for the matter the past. Evacuation of violence into someone else, is in analysis, a form of giving up on grief and movement. An inability to move forward with our onward development and hope. Inability to grieve and vengefulness are signs and symptoms, for Searles, of borderline conditions. One of the 'reliable criteria' of this diagnosis is a 'striking loss of memory – amnesia – for the events of his childhood'. The more extensive and powerful the amnesia, in Searles's view, the more powerfully 'he is unconsciously reliving his childhood in the transference-relationship with the analyst' (Searles, 1986, p. 297).

Vengeance comes in Toni Morrison's novel *Beloved*, in the form and spirit of a baby ghost: '124 was spiteful. Full of a bay's venom. The women in the house knew it and so did the children' (Morrison, 1987, p. 3). The novel opens with a description of house 124 and the spite living inside it which intimidates and bullies the women and children. And the spitefulness of the house is loaded, crammed to the rafters, like a baby's venom, with revenge. The ghost is the baby girl who was killed by her mother, to prevent the child being recaptured as a slave. *Beloved* is Morrison's act as a writer, to reclaim the history of slavery written up by the colonisers, to enable a more 'intimate' history for Black people. Slavery was a holocaust, the first holocaust according to Morrison situated at the origins of modernity, which no one wants to remember. In an interview just after the publication of the novel, Morrison registers surprise at the public interest in her book. She thought this would be the least read of all the books she had written because it was about 'Something the characters don't want to remember, white people don't want to remember. I mean its national amnesia' (Morrison, 1989).

The trauma of slavery is unspeakable because of the trauma and unspoken because, as Morrison says, the slaves, the characters in *Beloved* 'lived in a society and system in which the conquerors write the history of their lives' (Morrison, 2020c, p. 324). Because the slaves were the object not the subjects of history, memory was complicated. Morrison is interested and therefore makes us curious in what memory means for the characters in her novel; and, following on from this, the relationship between history and memory that we are all caught up in. What is memory exactly? How does it serve us? Are there memories we need to forget and more sustaining ones that generate growth? Is memory a factual truth or an imaginative fiction and how does that matter?

Because the history of slavery had been written up by white people there was a paucity of any reliable narratives for Toni Morrison to use as source material. Although there were many slave narratives written by actual slaves, the form and these narratives, often in the sentimental style of the day, kept many of the horrors of slavery hidden because these writers did not want to alienate the white readers who might be minded, to help. Whatever was chosen to be represented or veiled, Morrison became aware that the interior lives of the slaves were absent. Repeatedly the phrase 'But let us draw a veil over these proceedings too terrible to relate' appeared to occlude not just the picture of what happened but the way it was felt and experienced by the slaves themselves (Morrison, 2020b, p. 237). In her essay 'Unspeakable Things Unspoken', Morrison (2020a) explores the savagery of how a white imperialist culture has routinely removed and denied an Afro-American presence, its culture and art forms. So, in the absence of any kind of usable history, Morrison's literary archaeology has been to go back to the remnants of what can be found. She starts with an image or picture, elicited together with the 'act of the imagination' to make the memory work.

The historical remnant that formed the first image for Morrison in writing *Beloved* was an old newspaper clipping about a slave woman Margaret Garner who tried to murder her children, rather than seeing them being sold back into slavery. In the event she only succeeded in killing her two-year old daughter. What occurred to Morrison in reading the events surrounding Garner's act of infanticide was not so much the details of the case but what this act of murdering your own child said about the status of freedom for slaves. Garner was found not guilty on the basis that as a slave she was simply property, nonhuman. Thus, not being able to own her children and so not responsible for harming them. Considering the women's movement and the claim for the freedom of choice reproductively, Morrison wanted to explore how being a mother and a 'parent' for slaves was perhaps the most emancipatory claim of all. So, when it came to writing this repressed history, she was less interested in the facts than in how she could use them imaginatively.

Beloved holds an important place for me emotionally and historically. Although I am very clear that I am writing this as a white woman with the legacy of all that this means for writing about this singular text. Nevertheless, it was and remains a very important novel to me. I first read it before the start of my MA in literature at Sussex University, and it spoke to me in a powerful way. I was living in a chaotic housing cooperative and decided to move out of the lesbian section, as I had just given birth to my daughter and needed more privacy and quiet. I relocated to a hippie household round the corner, which was just as noisy, but had an attic floor. I had two small rooms and a shared kitchen. Adjacent to me lived a black, half-African man whom I became very close to during the first few months of my daughter's life. He gave me Morrison's book when my daughter was born because I had named her Esme, which means *Beloved* in French. We talked about the book and about racism in the UK, but what I recall most is the love and friendship between us, and how he helped me with my baby. My mother had been very committed to anti-racism and I had grown up under her tutelage; a follower of Martin Luther King, she educated me against antisemitism and racism. The racism towards my black friends, at school throughout my childhood was overt and, if I'm honest, frightening to me. Racism was rampant when I worked as a young woman in the NHS. I remember working as an agency midwife at a London training hospital and the white male consultant had gold stars on the notes for the women he would see. No one who was non-white or a single mother had notes with a gold star. One day, when he was working in the clinic, me and another agency staff nurse, probably being bold, because we were not permanent staff, put gold stars on all the notes. He went nuts. In retrospect our action was insensitive to all the non-white, single mothers who had to put up with his racism that day. But they were also being deprived of the expertise they had a right to. I guess the memory is illustrative of how open racism was in the early eighties.

The man I shared the attic with was called S. We shared histories and life stories, and his were harder, much harder and more traumatic than mine by virtue of his race. I remember he was the first man that taught my daughter to laugh, he would hold her up high, above his head, and then they would both laugh together. My love for him was inextricable from the love he showed my daughter. One of the things I have learnt many times before and after I read *Beloved*, was that my guilt was inadequate. Indeed, guilt about racism is not just inadequate, it's blinding, because it returns white people to a preoccupation with their own moral worth, rather than being able to see and understand, or listen to experiences of people who suffer racism on a daily basis. Guilt provokes fear and distance, it stops us being able to think or wonder about what makes racism so intractable and cruel, or what it means to be more entitled because of our skin colour. Is the guilt also because of the brutality this prejudice invites in all of us? Racism makes everyone psychotic, not just the victims but the perpetrators too, and so the terror it provokes in us and inflicts on other people will continue as long as we refuse to acknowledge what is happening.

Beloved spoke to me, in a way that pierced through the guilt I still unconsciously carried. The novel moved me emotionally, but it also moved something else fundamental in my understanding. Saying racism is bad or wrong doesn't address the structural inequalities in any society where servants and slaves are apparently needed to contain all the things about ourselves, we simply prefer not to look at. In Baldwin's analysis of *Uncle Tom's Cabin*, Stowe's virtuous rage is motivated by 'a terror of damnation', it's a fear, that in his view also drives the lynch mob (Baldwin, 1998, p. 14). The panic that racism unleashes, what Baldwin names as a 'fear of the dark' not only 'motivates our cruelty'; this panic imprisons all of us in differing ways:

> This fear of the dark makes it impossible that our lives shall be other than superficial; this, interlocked with and feeding our glittering, mechanical, inescapable civilisation which has put to death our freedom.
>
> (Baldwin, 1998, p. 15)

Morrison's *Beloved* has been the subject of many censorship wars advanced by right-wing republicans in the USA. Adults objecting to the effects the explicit sexual violence and brutality depicted will have on children. But of course, it's simply the brutality of a history, as Morrison says, no-one wants to remember.

Part Two

When it comes to histories, there are the ones that rule us, and the ones we prefer. And yet there are histories; internal as well as external lives that remain unknown and unheard. Are these stories unconscious because we don't want to remember them; or are they unconscious because they disturb or confront the governing cultures within which we are situated. The unconscious seems always in opposition to the authorities, whether they are placed within or without. Does reparation really help unearth these hidden or forgotten histories? How do we make reparations for slavery for example? We can't heal the brutality or the violence of that unspeakable past. Is reparation even the right word to think of how we make financial compensations or more radically give back stolen and occupied lands? And what would indigenous people want from the colonial cultures that have plundered so much? In *Dancing on our Turtle's Back: Stories of Nishnaabeg Recreation, Resurgence and a New Emergency*, Leanna Betasamosake Simpson (2011) describes the oral story telling of her people (or Nishnaabeg). These stories which are reciprocally exchanged between families and groups of indigenous people are encounters between humans and plants, or animal nations, where mutual respect and responsibility are beneficial to both sides. Simpson does not call these stories reparative. Rather they are a resurgence of cultural forms, that have been negated by colonial powers. Stories, here, are a praxis, and the exchanges that are made are treaties. Breast-feeding is one of the first treaties, where the child learns about sharing in a treaty that benefits both sides. For this treaty to work, mother and child must be looked after, so gentleness and care can be given to raising the child. This first treaty gives way to wider forms of communication within the community and then with reciprocal treaties with other nations outside. Simpson is critical of the various offers of reconciliation made by the Canadian state, or government bodies to her people. Because Canadian people don't understand the ongoing injustice of occupation and dispossession of lands (belonging to the Nishnaabeg), treaty negotiations have failed. Simpson compares these offers of reconciliation to an abusive relationship, where the perpetrator wants to reconcile, and the partner can't, without risking more abuse. Reparation is rather like this notion of reconciliation, not just because it is idealistic. But because it rests on the assumption you can heal and repair the past when you simply can't.

Simpson's stories of breastfeeding as a cultural exchange, that is both internal and external, are rather different to Melanie Klein's description of reparation to the breast for the damage done. For Klein was simply not interested in how the baby and mother get along together in a real way. Internal reparation is integral to Klein's most famous idea of the depressive position. Split between the love and hate of their early objects or parents, children experience persecutory hate associated with frustration oscillating with a more reparative love aimed at restoring the injured object. This movement as Klein herself acknowledges, is often more of a stand-off, with obsessional desires of reparation being inseparable from the manic omnipotent defences that want to control and cut the object down to size:

> The desire to control the object, the sadistic gratification of overcoming and humiliating it, of getting the better of it, the *triumph* over it, may enter so strongly into the act of reparation (carried out by thoughts, activities or sublimations) that the 'benign' circle started by this act becomes broken. The objects which were to be restored change again into persecutors, and in turn paranoid fears

are revived. These fears reinforce the paranoid defence mechanisms (of destroying the object) ... The reparation that was in progress is thus disturbed of nullified ... As a result of the failure of the act of reparation, the ego has to resort again and again to obsessional defences.

(Klein, 1998, p. 351)

What Klein is describing is a circle of how reparation operates, and seemingly how it can never work. Describing the difficulty children can feel and find in developing into adults, Klein explains the source as the unconscious guilt and triumph they feel about their parents. Thus, Oedipal fantasies of rivalry lead children to feelings of triumph over their parents, and the guilt that arises thwarts the reparative love to those parental objects. For example, not being able to succeed in life can be a consequence of this guilt, because the fear of damage to the parents is too high. Depression can be a result of these conflicts, as well as manic defences. So, what moves this stand-off between love and hate from Klein's point of view? How does the ego finally overcome the conflict inherent, within the depressive position? Paradoxically, Klein is at her most interesting when she describes, all the differing ways reparation to the loved object is stymied, or reversed, into its opposite.

Apart from depression and a sadistic control of the humiliated object, hypomania and obsession prevail. A hypomanic person will idealise and devalue objects or other people. Boasting, exaggerating their importance and being contemptuous of conscientiousness and detail, the hypomanic character can change or switch to display the opposite symptoms of obsessional fixation on methods and details. All of this contempt and denial is a defence against mourning for the mother. And yet although these might not appear particularly attractive descriptions; they are very ordinary ones we can spot, daily, in ourselves and others. So, how do we manage to overcome the depressive position in Klein's view? At this point she becomes extremely vague and suggests that normal growing up, testing reality, the development and sublimation of skills and talents lead us to master our bad persecutory objects. But how exactly, and what if this isn't ultimately fruitful?

Klein writes:

When the child's belief and trust in his capacity to love, in his reparative powers and in the integration and security of his good inner world increase as a result of the constant and manifold proofs and counterproofs gained by the testing of external reality, manic omnipotence decreases and the obsessional nature of the impulses toward reparation, which means in general that the infantile neurosis has passed.

(Klein, 1998, p. 353)

But doesn't all reparation contain or be a consequence of guilt? So, given that this must be true, how to we ever really piece together the degrees of separation between our obsessive guilty reparations and our more loving ones? Why does love in relation to our internal people or parents always have been marked so indelibly with guilt. Can't we have love as a pleasure, and dependence on the object which is grateful for what it's given and not always on some backslide into persecution? And what makes the difference? Is it a difference between obligatory love, a sort of meal ticket, where past greediness has to be atoned for. A reparation, in other words, that simply returns us to old wounds, the furious and frustrated deprivation, that we can't ditch. Or, on the other hand, a love that comes from bearing that frustration, not because we have repaired it or found absolution for our past injuries and crimes. A frustration that can be borne because the love it gets is good enough to keep waiting for, or seeking out. Love, as it were, not as reparative or guilty; intimacy that has learnt how giving and receiving pleasure is enjoyable on its own terms. Love, perhaps, that doesn't have to be a trade-off. Of course, for this passion or tenderness to come about, the frustrations of not getting what we want, Klein's paranoid-schizoid position, must be tolerated. Love tests to reality can work backwards and forwards. And they work best when they are a truly a jump of faith into something startling, where there are no guarantees.

   Love that is always suspicious, and carries an unconscious demand for restitution rarely works, because it is so likely to fail or be disappointed; to fall backwards into the circle of reparation, that Klein so vividly describes. This is poisonous hope because it is destined to be thwarted at every turn. So, we have to careful with our understanding of reparation, as it can so easily become a roundabout that returns us back to are original rage and triumph rather than onwards to what may be surprising to us, in relation to ourselves, but also to a wider world. The problem of course is, how exactly can we love without entitlement or expectation? An entitlement that can't just be explained by psychoanalysis. Growing up, Klein suggests, is the solution to our 'infantile neurosis'. But what mature development means is so different depending on culture and context. And arguably no-one grows up if they live in a society that is organised between those that are entitled to the goods, and those that aren't. Or in Baldwin's terms, as long as society categorises us into whom is superior or inferior, racially pure or dark, we are all bound, externally and then psychologically. Although he describes how slaves and their descendants, who have been invented to serve their colonial oppressors, become written up and defined, their humanity denied by the cruelty of their so called 'owners'. He is also making the wider point, that no-one escapes society's categorisation.

In other words, none of us are really free so long as the structure of our culture betrays anyone's community their true humanity:

> We take our shape, it is true, within and against that cage of reality bequeathed us at birth, and yet it is precisely through our dependence on this reality that we are most endlessly betrayed. ... Within this cage it is romantic, more, meaningless, to speak of a 'new' society as the desire of the oppressed, for that shivering dependence with the *Herrenvolk* makes a truly 'new' society impossible to conceive.
>
> (Baldwin, 1998, p. 16)

One thing is certain, privilege and entitlement which the governing elite elide with progress, does nothing to prevent inequality, cruelty and aggression; in fact, it is precisely these acquisitions or 'achievements' for the few that means more harsh deprivation for the many. We can't, as many psychoanalysts want to, analyse individual violence without reference to the cultural cage, as Baldwin states, that we are endlessly thrown back against. I was talking to a nurse from the Philippines recently, working in Brighton. Her training included pharmacology, mental health nurse training and midwifery. A training that far exceeds what British nurses undergo, and yet she can't make ends meet and must work on all her days off, to survive and save a little. Why that doesn't make her (and everyone) angrier I have no idea.

If reparation is a circle that can't move forward, how do we move beyond trauma or neurosis to the future? How do we break free, at least in part, from repetition of the cultural cage that Baldwin so eloquently describes? Freud wrote remarkably little about clinical technique, and maybe that can be seen as a regenerative impulse to therapists today, to experiment and make things up. As hopefully many psychoanalysts know, there is no right way to be a therapist, any-more than there is a right way to be a person. In his classic essay 'Remembering, Repeating and Working Through', Freud describes how remembering and discharging repressed memories through hypnosis gave way to free association and interpretation of the transference. The later method revealed how repressed memories were acted out in the present moment in relation to the transference.

> We may say that the patient does not remember anything of what he has forgotten or repressed but acts it out. He reproduces it not as a memory but as an action; he repeats it, without, of course knowing that he is repeating it. For instance, the patient does not say that he

used to be defiant and critical towards his parent's authority; instead
he behaves that way to the doctor.

(Freud, 1914, p. 150)

Repeating replaces remembering, and the strength of acting out is the
clue to the durability of the patient's defences. But these defences, what
Freud calls the 'armoury of the past', are 'weapons' against the treatment
that the therapist must grapple with and 'wrest away' gradually from the
client. Freud acknowledges much like his daughter, that time and patience
has to be taken with the patient, to 'work through' the resistances. Some
of this is very true, and it is natural for people when they have made
progress to revert backwards before they move forward again. Habits are
hard to break, and the old solutions are familiar and dear. But of course,
there are at least, two obvious problems with Freud arguments. Remembering does not, on its own, promise any change in therapy. People
remember the same stuff over and over; we all do, without necessarily
moving forward. And defences are not bad things, they are necessary
imaginative tools with which we clothe the ego and enable it to move.
Being rebellious against your therapist's authority ought to be seen as a
genuinely healthy characteristic. Authority, scaring someone into compliance, rarely succeeds, in childhood or any time after.

Trauma, in my experience, isn't moved by simply remembering.
Sometimes when the trauma is severe, when you have had too much of a
past to recover from, as in childhood abuse, the past is as Morrison
would put it 'unspeakable'. To move or change we need more imagination of what can be new or different. Working through trauma, in my
experience, if that just means remembering it, isn't enough. Paucity of
trauma memories their literal nature, makes elaboration difficult. And it
is precisely Freud's basic rule of free association that then finds resistance. Because people don't want to remember, but also because the
memories are in themselves very impoverished and static. It is as if,
when experience is traumatic and overwhelming, memories don't get laid
down in the same way. They may consist of images, or sounds, but a
fully expanded story is missing. The more traumas there are, the more
gaps and erasures. And so, this raises a very interesting discussion of
what memory is, and whether it works without more help from the
imagination. Thus, even Freud's 'Remembering, Repeating and Working
Through' can't move forward without a creative power to the memory,
or the events in question.

But of course, the way memories come to life, is through the telling,
between the writer and the reader, or between the patient and the analyst. The stories, if you like, that happen in this alive manner, are made

up through the praxis of at least two people shaping this fictionalised version of the facts, between them. Memories, like emotions have to be shared to be felt in a meaningful way. For Morrison, the scraps of memory, what we might call the facts, are less important than the imaginative work of what she calls 'rememory'; the imagistic and metaphorical associations involved in remembering the past. I have for a long time, from the beginning of my career as a therapist, been influenced by this idea of rememory, because it adds something to Freud's method of free association. But for it to operate, free association has to be something that both analyst and patient participate in. It was with her novel *Beloved* that Morrison's ideas of memory came together. And what she says about it is this:

> Rememory as in recollecting and remembering, as in reassembling the members of the body, the family, the population of the past. And it was the struggle, the pitched battle between remembering and forgetting that became the device of the narrative.
>
> (Morrison, 2020b, p. 234)

The characters in *Beloved* don't want to remember what has been unbearable, so they forget, but they can't avoid the past either, as it bumps into them at every turn. History cannot help them because it has been written up by the 'conquerors', and so the stories that are shared or kept secret between the different people in the book, are not just a recollection they are a 'doing'; an action which reconstitutes or makes anew what has previously been unavailable.

This practice is conveyed in the book by different tales. There are stories that Sethe's youngest daughter, Denver, longs for about her origins and ancestors, but are kept short by her mother. When the baby ghost of Sethe's dead daughter turns up in real life, she is a beautiful young woman. This ghost is greedy for Sethe's stories of the past. Searching her mother's face, Beloved smiles her wide smile and asks Sethe to tell the story about her diamonds. Stories from Sethe become a way to feed Beloved, just like a mother feeds her children milk. And this is wondrous for Sethe, because as much as it pained her to revisit the past, everything in it was wounded or lost; what hurt her seemed to deeply fill and satisfy her daughter. The diamonds were the crystal earrings the slave-owner's wife had given Sethe when she got married in captivity. And, of course because of the associative nature of memory the earrings opened up a past that Sethe couldn't bear to go back to. Over time, though, because of Beloved's 'thirst' for the telling, the act becomes a surprising pleasure for Sethe too. And yet, the generative storytelling between Beloved and Sethe ceases and descends into a cycle of Beloved's endless demands and Sethe's guilty and hopeless attempts to satisfy her. Nothing, Sethe does to atone is enough. The atmosphere changes, slowly and then more rapidly, as the arguing begins. Beloved makes a complaint and Sethe apologises, acts of kindness from the mother are ignored or dismissed, until the orders begin and Beloved just barks 'do it'. In response, her appeasing mother meekly complies. As this violent reparative circle continues, Sethe becomes so exhausted and thin, Denver realises she must act, otherwise her mother will die. Her whole world, encompassed by the other women in the house, is something Denver must leave, and step outside of. She will have to go and ask somebody in the community for help.

Morrison can't rely on historical accounts of the past in relation to slavery, and neither can a white literary history help her. So autobiographical accounts of slaves are useful, together with her own family memories. Avoidance of received history, the data of it, is two-fold in Morrison's writing. First, because accepted histories of Slavery, however brutal, have become accepted by the reader and not questioned. The terribleness of it becomes unremarkable. Once we become accustomed to awful things, we can be unsurprised by them, and this is a problem. But the concept of memory (or rememory) that then takes precedence for Morrison, over history, is one that can improvise and ignite the imagination and entails the involvement and attention of the reader.

One obvious example of this today is the Post Office scandal in the UK, which started around 1999, the biggest miscarriage of justice in living history, which was ignored by seemingly everybody. When ITV broadcast a film of this and made it into a living, interior story from the perspective of the victims of the crime, that spoke to the viewers, this unheard history changed. Becoming alive as rememory because it moved a nation of people emotionally. No doubt these events also spoke to many people's experiences of the corruptness of governance in this country at the present time. But what was for many, just one amongst the many accepted accounts of corruption by those in power, came to life in the story that was told on screen.

Morrison attends to the explicit difficulties of writing about race into today's society. She is writing, what she calls, 'a more intimate form of history', one that will escape from the dangers of falling into a received narrative, that everybody either ignores, or turns into voyeurism. And for that task she employs a kind of impressionistic approach. She describes this by comparing it to looking at a painting of listening to a piece of music without reference to the surrounding literary criticism. You can go to the Tate Britain or Tate Modern in London and read all the detail which has helped choreograph the paintings. Or you can just wander about and see and feel how they land with you. Describing such a painterly memory from her childhood, Morrison recalls some impressions of a woman she didn't know well, called Hannah Peace: 'the colour of her skin, – the matte quality of it. Something purple around her. Also eyes not completely open' (Morrison, 2020d, p. 327). And yet for Morrison this sensory but vague memory is more helpful than too much factual knowledge or features that might interfere with the subsequent imagining of this woman for characterisation in her novel *Sula*. She writes: 'What is useful – definitive – is the galaxy of emotion that accompanied the woman as I pursued my memory of her; not the woman herself' (Morrison, 2020d, p. 327).

In therapy, the received history that the patient brings as a preferred self, how she or he or they have been situated by families and cultural experiences is often what first is encountered as the case history, with all the symptoms of that history, or the identity, that have worked to acclimatise and perhaps deaden the person to his pain. We call these symptoms of history, defences. And so, putting these symptoms into correspondence or conversation is a way of involving both the analyst and patient into what can be both imaginative and startling. It is not just the creative memory of the patient that is invoked but the re-memory of the analyst, her creative associations that clearly leads back to her own past, and not just who she is listening to. The surprise of a therapy session has to lead away from a storytelling that is rehearsed, like the ones dragged and encountered in boring middle-class dinner party conversations. And the feelings that become aroused, are on both sides of the therapeutic encounter. What is evoked, then, is central to the rememory that is occurring between both participants.

As an act of willed and unconscious creation, memory becomes unearthing something new, rather than what is expected or too familiar. Hope, perhaps, depends on this creative memory, an act of storytelling that can be an ongoing exchange, rather than the restoration of old wounds and histories. We could think of therapy as a bit like a geographical map, that we re-make up as we go along, rather than a past that has to be re-circulated. Hence, the maps in Richard's analysis with Klein were overdetermined by what she was telling him. If she could of, listened more to what else he could draw from his own imagination, and also what she might in turn draw, then the therapy might have been very different. Who knows what maps of memory might have been created? Klein was very aware of Richard's anxieties about the war and his own aggression. But for her, the war, outside, was merely a reflection of the instinctual war going on inside. Aggression has always been a difficult topic for psychoanalysis to address. Although it was seen as running parallel to the libidinal drives; the successful fusion of the love and hate at the Oedipal stage, and an ability to bear the conflict between these two forces, remained inadequate to explain the virulence of people's destructiveness. And it was an awareness of this, together with a world war, that pre-empted Freud's creation of the death drive.

Taking up on the death drive with alacrity, Klein used it to describe the primitive anxieties of small children, like Richard. But why do small children's minds have to be a map of war, why can't they also contain maps of grief and peace? And let's remind ourselves that reparation is not part of this. The whole point of a map is that it leads somewhere new; we use it to navigate our path. Anna Freud had plenty of different territories and maps of the mind, and her psychic geography was not just limited to ego, id and superego. She listed at least ten ego defences, many of which are unconscious. Anna Freud did not believe you could analyse children in the same way as adults, because the transference is always split with the parents. Moreover, children's super-egos are not mature or separate enough to withstand transference interpretations. Neither did she believe that children free-associate in the way adults do. Toys and actions aren't words. And yet imagination is something children and adults can share.

Is aggression a defence or an instinct? Is it part of the id or the controlling ego? Aggression as Anna Freud acknowledges has a healthy part of everybody's development. Without it we would not survive separation, we would not sublimate and learn new skills. We would not be able to compete, or grow-up, have gratifying sexual relationships and so on. What is the relationship between imagination and aggression? When it comes to wars, it seems that aggression starts where more imaginative conversation stops. And yet the blending of aggression with love in a primitive state was what the artist and psychoanalyst Marion Milner was absorbed with. For her, love could not come into being without hate, which created necessary separateness and form. The artist, Milner tells us, and the psychoanalyst, have a shared project in creativity; by moving from a primitive state of fusion (Freud's oceanic feeling), towards more external boundaries of the self or reality, and then back again. This oscillation between unconscious fantasy and the ego reality of a more outside world, is the space of poetry and illusion. Poetic illusion is what Milner understood Freud to be talking about in his concept of free association, but he refrained on elaborating further. In Milner's view, Freud became so interested in 'the content of unconscious phantasies he neglected their form'. In her wonderful essay *Psychoanalysis and Art* (1956) Milner describes how illusion gives way to symbol formation, where the idea of the primary thing is temporarily, 'merged with the idea of a substitute'. Loss becomes a crucial aspect of this creative process; the loss of the omnipotence of that primary illusion being, 'an essential aspect of symbol formation' (Milner, 2002, p. 208).

For Milner, the death-drive is the destructiveness that can arise as a frustrated and distorted form of 'the self-surrender which is inherent in the creative process'. The death-drive is then, an inability to grieve our omnipotence or to have illusions which need to then lose, or in part be given up, to make way for the path of imagination. To give Klein and her followers their due, the creative links between aggression and symbol formation were part of their thinking. But Klein's focus on the death-drive and reparation stilts the movement of forms, and misses the creative fluidity, that Milner manages to name. Illusion, then, and its loss, as a kind of continual movement between the creative aspects of the unconscious and the rational mind, is a way of creating new forms and identities, by connecting us to the unconscious sameness and similarities between ourselves and others. As Milner writes:

> The unconscious mind, by the very fact of its not clinging to the distinction between self and other, seer and seen, can do things the conscious logical mind can not do. By being more sensitive to the sameness's rather than the differences between things, by being passionately concerned with finding 'the familiar in the unfamiliar'.
>
> (Milner, 2002, p. 214)

So, this fusion and movement that Milner traces between the unconscious and the external world, unforming and forming, synthesises our aggression, with poetry or creativity. This is, for Milner, the source 'for all renewal and rebirth'. We could wonder, if such movement of finding similarity within difference could be the fragile path towards a hope that is not omniscient.

The ego has fallen out of favour in recent post-Lacanian times. But reading Anna Freud's work on *The Ego and the Mechanisms of Defence*, one is struck by all the different aspects of the personality ego defences refer to. The ego is not just some unified essentialism located in the imaginary, as Lacan would propose. It ranges from rigidity to flexibility, awareness to unknowability. The ego, and its parts, can be seen as more than rigid straitjackets keeping things down and out. Ego forms, have the potential to open unconsciously or unfurl as more poetic forms. Anna Freud notes, quoting James Strachey, that the ego in therapy 'has to be made more tolerant'. But arguably the key is in making the ego unfold artistically, allowing it entry into the poetic experience that Milner describes. Imagination, then as neither too much, aggression, or too much inhibition.

Rememory, as Toni Morrison describes it, would be seen not so much as a defence, but as an art form of the ego, which allows emotion and imagination to move us into a more alive encounter, not just with the past, but also the future. This memory, as Morrison reminds us, is primarily more painterly or musical than linguistic. It moves from image or picture, to meaning or symbol, and then the text. In the analytic session we use fragments of dreams, much like Morrison's memory of Hannah Peace, and through imaginative association we create, and work back and forwards to enable dream narratives. Dreams are always about both our past and our future and they are always linked to what is going on in the therapy.

But the imagistic memory of Hannah Peace reminds me most clearly of Freud's paper 'Screen Memories'. James Strachey notes, in his introduction, that in this original account of screen memories, the earlier more innocent image can act as a cover for a later memory. Over time, this early to later movement of the screen memory is lost and the meaning is simply an innocuous image screening over an earlier significant childhood event. As Strachey says:

> It is a curious thing that the type of screen memory mainly considered in the present – one in which an early memory is used as a screen for a later event – almost disappears from later literature. What has since come to be regarded as the regular type – one in which an early event is screened by a later memory – is only barely alluded to here.
>
> (James Strachey in Freud, 1899, p. 302)

The paper, which was written in relation to Freud's own autobiographical therapy, describes three scenes from his early childhood and young adulthood. In the childhood scene Freud who is 2–3 years old is on a patch of meadow and playing with his young cousins, a girl and a boy. They are picking bright yellow flowers – dandelions – and the girl has the biggest bunch, so the boys steal them. A peasant woman in a nearby house comforts the girl with some newly baked black bread. The greedy boys ask for some too, and on being given some, throw their flowers away. Freud remembers the wonderful taste of the bread as almost hallucinogenic, and the yellow of the flowers as vibrant. Freud moves away soon after from his birthplace in the provinces, to the town because of a downturn in his father's fortunes. The second scene is Freud at the age of 17 years returning to the country to visit family friends. He falls in love with a young woman in a yellow dress, who is around for a bit and then disappears back to school after the holidays. Leaving him longing after her. He walks nostalgically in the woods building 'castles in the air' of what could have been, between them. The yellow colour of her dress haunts him. As Freud notes, his fantasies at the time were not about the future, 'but sought to improve the past. If only the smash had not occurred', meaning the dramatic loss of Freud's father's livelihood. If only the family had stayed in the country when he was little, and he had grown strong near his friends, her brothers, he would be following in his father's footsteps and marrying the girl of his dreams. This was despite the fact Freud has always fled from his father's ambitions for him. The 'other' Freud, his interlocutor in the self-analysis or exchange, joins in, and reminds him of the earlier memory: 'Do you not suspect that there may be a connection with the colour of the girl's dress and the ultra-clear yellow of the flowers in your childhood scene?' (Freud, 1899, p. 313). Could it be that the dandelion girl and following the 'bread and butter' occupation of his father's profession is what Freud is lovesick about, in the second memory, the missing life, that could have prevailed? 'Possibly,' considers Freud, 'but it was not the same yellow. The dress was more of a yellowish brown, more like the colour of wall flowers' (Freud, 1899, pp. 313–314).

Disagreeing with his negotiator (or analyst), Freud notes the darker colour of the dress in contrast to the original dandelions, and then associates this richer shade with the mountain flowers he encountered on his walks whilst at university. This wields into view the last scene, of Freud bumping into his female cousin, a few years after his passion for the girl in the yellow dress. In retrospect he is aware of a scheme by his father, and uncle, to marry him off to her. And yet, Freud remains indifferent and resistant, as he is bent on his university studies. He remembers the alpine strolls as the only luxury he avails himself with his work and the dark yellow flowers he sees growing there. In the analysis or storytelling that Freud enacts with himself he traces the yellow flowers between the three memories. It is the darker yellow of the alpine flowers in the last fantasy that are truly reminiscent of Freud's passion for the girl in the dress. These mountain flowers represent Freud's repressed desires, traced backwards. To deflower the young cousin, stealing her dandelions, which are a mere 'flowery defence'. And forwards, the flowers become a re-memory of his truest ideals. His desire through university and onward to his chosen vocation as an analyst.

The storytelling in 'Screen Memories' between two parts of Freud's self is a series of negotiations (or treaties) that move Freud from his past to his future. They are not simply recollections but a form of re-memory that imaginatively puts the memories into action and propels them forth to what is indeed Freud's realisable hope. The treaties in his self-analysis, between the different sides of himself don't always work out. For example, the treaty with the super-ego that is telling him he should have settled down with the country girl and become a doctor like his dad. Reparation to his father and his past is not Freud's solution, to the Oedipal complex or anything beyond it. Follow the yellow flowers, Freud tells himself, and us, if you want to get to your future. Redrawing the same old Oedipal map can't move or change his life. It is the flowers as unfolding ego forms, through which Freud moves; the re-memory which helps Freud creatively imagine a new path and walk on through it.

We can also think of Freud's analysis of the flowers as both illusory images (or fantasies) that move through storytelling from unconscious similarity to a more symbolic form. In other words, it is the poetry of Freud's unknowable selves that enable the renewal of his personal history. Hope, today, is everywhere to be looked for, and seemingly nowhere to be found. Violence has become a nostalgic rhetoric of how we repair are pasts, as if it is through this repair that we can finally be liberated and leave when actually nothing could be further from the truth. When the trauma is too great, grieving becomes seemingly impossible. How can we bear to voluntary lose, what we feel was taken from us in such a brutal fashion? And so move between forgetfulness and remembering? Between, on the one hand, a resistance, not so much to the past but to our refusal to leave it; how, it has taken up within us a permanent melancholia or haunting. And, on the other, a reimagination of a more liveable destiny.

What shapes can we recreate, to make hope something alive and shifting enough to surprise us away from the accepted categories or identities we currently live within? Not as a false ideal, that will beckon us back to a reparative fantasy which is familiar but ultimately leads nowhere – to a dead end. Talking of shapes and maps, the solution to the Israel–Hamas war, arguably entails one big redrawing of maps. What would it take for that killing rage to find some similarities amidst so many deathly boundaries of difference? And maybe this is how we see realistic hope as working. Not as something that has an investment in a history that is too accepted and therefore too immovable There is unimaginable pain involved on both sides and histories in Israel's war with Hamas. Terrorist violence and genocide, are quite obviously, not about any form of peace or reconciliation. Hope, like history, comes in many guises or varieties, but for it to be true it has to move forward, not as an idealistic or nostalgic fantasy but as a living, poetic, re-creation. Freud found that when it came to formative times, his childhood fantasies were insufficient. What enabled him to break away from his reparative past, and possibly his rage for what his family had been deprived of, was to marry, not his father's ideals, but his historical hope with a burgeoning desire to have a new tomorrow. History has perhaps made psychoanalysis too pedestrian, there is too much homage and reparation to its supposed origins and ancestors; with not enough attention to what we can differently dream up. Psychoanalysis, much like the world we find ourselves in, has to follow the intuition and the colours of the imagination, for we might have little else. To envisage a future that isn't always returning through the back door to our past. And to differently negotiate our 'cultural cage', with all the hurtful shame and sadomasochism attached to it, we have to take risks. For hope, if it's to be more than 'castles in the air', has to undo us, in a renewal of what is accepted as history, personal or otherwise. It has to broker what we might not know, until we potentially find it with the help of each other. Maybe, the last words must go to James Baldwin; when asked in a television interview if he is still in despair about the world, Baldwin replies, in the negative, that he has been enraged by the world but not despairing: 'I can't afford despair, I can't tell my nephew, my niece. You can't tell the children there is no hope' (Baldwin, 1987).

References

Baldwin, J. (1998) Everybody's Protest Novel, in *James Baldwin: Collected Essays*, pp. 11–18, New York, Library of America.

Baldwin, J. (1987) James Baldwin interview with Mavis Nicholson, aired 12 February, retrieved from www.youtube.com/watch?v=KolocnMkdYk.

Freedland, J. (2023) Too Many Taking Sides in This Conflict Miss the True Nature of Hamas – and Netanyahu, *The Guardian*, 17 November, retrieved from www.theguardian.com/commentisfree/2023/nov/17/hamas-benjamin-netanyahu-ceasefire.

Freud, A. (1971) Problems of Psychoanalytic Training, Diagnosis, and the Technique of Therapy, in *The Writings of Anna Freud*, vol. VII, New York, International Universities Press.

Freud, A. (1974) The Ego and the Mechanisms of Defence, in *The Writings of Anna Freud*, vol. II, New York, International Universities Press.

Freud, S. (1899) Screen Memories, in *The Standard Edition of the Complete Psychological Works of Sigmund Freud*, volume 3, translated by J. Strachey, London, Hogarth Press.

Freud, S. (1914) Remembering, Repeating and Working Through, in *The Standard Edition of the Complete Psychological Works of Sigmund Freud*, volume 12, translated by J. Strachey, London, Hogarth Press.

Klein, M. (1998) *Narrative of a Child Analysis: The Conduct of the Psycho-Analysis of Children as seen in the Treatment of a Ten-year-old Boy*, London, Vintage.

Klein, M. (1998) Mourning and Its Relation to Manic Depressive States, in *Love, Guilt and Reparation*, introduction by H. Segal, pp. 344–369, London, Vintage.

Milner, M. (2002) Psychoanalysis and Art, in *the Suppressed Madness of Sane Men: Forty-Four Years of Exploring Psychoanalysis*, pp. 192–215, New York, Routledge.

Morrison, T. (1987) *Beloved*, London, Chatto and Windus.

Morrison, T. (1989), *The Pain of Being Black*, interview with B. Angelo, *Time Magazine*, 22 May.

Morrison, T. (2020a) Unspeakable Things Unspoken: The Afro-American Presence in American Literature, in *The Source of Self-Regard: Selected Essays, Speeches, and Meditations*, pp. 161–197, New York, Vintage Books.

Morrison, T. (2020b) The Site of Memory, in *The Source of Self-Regard*, pp. 233–245, New York, Vintage Books.

Morrison, T. (2020c) Rememory, in *The Source of Self-Regard*, pp. 322–325, New York, Vintage Books.

Morrison, T. (2020d) Memory, Creation and Fiction, in *The Source of Self-Regard*, pp. 326–333, New York, Vintage Books.

Said, E. (1994) Freedom from Domination in the Future, in *Culture and Imperialism*, pp. 341–408, London, Vintage Books.

Searles, H.F. (1986) The Psychodynamics of Vengefulness (1956), in *Collected Papers on Schizophrenia and Related Subjects*, London, Karnac Books.

Simpson, L. B. (2011) *Dancing on our Turtle's Back: Stories of Nishnaaberg Recreation, Resurgence and a New Emergency*, Winnipeg, Arbeiter Ring Publishing.

Index

protection from 116; racial 124; as
repression 116–117; reproduction of
119; restitution for 121; return to
114, 117; of slavery 122–123;
working through 129, 130
treatment compliance 119
Trotter, David 11
Trump, Donald 106

Ukraine 9
Uncle Tom's Cabin (Stowe) 114, 125
unconscious 114, 115–116, 117, 120,
122, 125, 135
University of Birmingham 97–98
unpleasure 49–52
'Unspeakable Things Unspoken' 123
utopias 2, 13

vengefulness 121–122
violence: and ego ideals 19; evacuation
of 122; Freud on 5; in Gaza 113,
117, 120–121, 138; individual 129;
as nostalgic rhetoric 138; of the past
125; sexual 28, 46, 125; terrorist
138; uncontrolled 71; in the
Western world 39
Virgin Mary 57, 58, 60

Walking Backwards into the Future
75–76
wealth inequality 5
Weil, Simone 62
Weinstein, Harvey 27–28
welfare state 75, 79
Welldon, Estela 65–67, 68–69
Wessely, Simon 82, 84, 89, 91–92, 93,
94–95, 96, 97, 102

White, Peter 96
Williams, Raymond 75–76
Wings of a Dove (James) 104
Winnicott, D. W.: on culture 78;
'Delinquency as a Sign of Hope'
71–72; on dependency 77; on
depression 5; on friendship 23; on
hope 59, 64–65, 73; on living 52; on
the mother-child relationship
14–15, 23, 50, 64–65, 75; on play 51,
73–74; on reality 9; on screaming
59; 'Transitional Objects and
Transitional Phenomena' 64
women: abused 3–4, 7; communities
of 36; desires of 6–7; development
of 66; domination of 44–45; emancipation of 55; as feminists 36–37;
idealisation of 59–60; and illness 81;
independent 43; Madonna/Whore
division 7, 38, 65–66; masochistic
49; as mother of hope 57–58, 78, 79;
and the mother-child relationship
14–15, 23, 50, 60–61, 64–66, 72, 75,
76, 116; as mothers 59–60, 62,
65–70, 73; as mothers of hope
57–58, 78–79; as murderers 66,
67–68; and pornography 38–39;
resilience of 27; and sacrifice 60;
sadistic 46; sexual desires of 7, 11,
41–42; sexual violence against
27–28; and shame 27–28; as slaves
123, 125, 132; in therapy 47; violence against 31; as wives 77
'Women's Time' (Kristeva) 60
Woolf, Leonard 102
Woolf, Virginia 95, 98, 102
World War II 118–119, 134

For Product Safety Concerns and Information please contact our EU
representative GPSR@taylorandfrancis.com
Taylor & Francis Verlag GmbH, Kaufingerstraße 24, 80331 München, Germany

* 9 7 8 1 0 3 2 8 4 9 5 1 5 *